Make Mathematics Your Best Friend

Make Mathematics Your Best Friend

Rajesh Kumar Thakur

B.Sc. (Maths Hons.) M.Sc. (Maths)
M.Sc. (Operation Research)
M.A. (Education), ETE, B.Ed.

Ocean Books Pvt. Ltd.
ISO 9001:2015 Publishers

Published by
Ocean Books (P) Ltd.
4/19 Asaf Ali Road,
New Delhi-110 002 (INDIA)
e-mail: info@oceanbooks.in

ISBN 978-81-8430-509-8
MAKE MATHEMATICS YOUR BEST FRIEND
by Rajesh Kumar Thakur

Edition
2025

Price
₹ 400.00 (Rupees Four Hundred Only)

Printed at
R-Tech Offset Printers, Delhi

This little book is dedicated to

India's greatest mathematical genius

Srinivas Iyengar Ramanujan

for his contribution

in the field of numbers.

PREFACE

A noted mathematician, C.F. Gauss has said: "Mathematics is the queen of all subjects".

Mastering mathematics does not require any otherworldly genius. A recent survey conducted by National Council of Educational Research and Training (NCERT) shows that more than 50% students of primary school do not have even the basic knowledge of the four fundamentals of mathematics, i.e. addition, subtraction, multiplication and division.

Most of us are of the same opinion — make the fundamentals clear and mathematics is yours. But what are the fundamentals of mathematics?

Being a teacher of mathematics, I noted the main reason behind this phobia for mathematics is that students are instructed to *learn* the numerous formulae, theorems, etc, without being explained the basic reasoning.

Suppose you are invited to dine with your friends and are served a variety of new dishes. The first question you will ask your friend is the name of the dish and how is it prepared. The same logic exists with mathematics. If your teacher serves you different formulae, theorems, equations, etc, on a big plate called blackboard, you are certainly not going to take it without having your doubts of *why* and *how* made clear.

I still remember, when in class 6 I was reprimanded by my mathematics teacher for asking why —x—= +. In class 10,

I was puzzled when I noticed $\frac{1}{0} = \infty$ (not defined) whereas $\frac{0}{1} = 0$. Such questions kept coming in my mind but I never got any satisfactory answer.

Let me ask you something about the greatest scientist Albert Einstein. How many of you know that he failed in mathematics when he was in class 6?

Einstein was very poor in Algebra so he could not score even the minimum pass percentage. His maternal uncle took the responsibility of teaching him Algebra. He took him to a nearby jungle and asked him to look at the sky and name the bird that was flying. Einstein was silent. His uncle took out a gun and fired a bullet. The bird fell down nearby. His uncle said: Let the bird killed be X, and went towards the place where the bird had fallen. They noticed that the bird was a crow. He said to Einstein that X = crow.

This simple logic that Algebra is the ladder to know the unknown made everything clear to Einstein.

Will you believe me if I say that at the age of 8, Gauss found the formula to sum the n terms in an Arithmetic Progression? Once his class teacher wrote on the blackboard—Find the sum of all numbers from 1 to 100. Gauss noticed that there are 50 such pairs each equal to 101 in between $1 + 2 + 3 + ... + 100$, so he multiplied 101×50 and got the answer 5050.

$1 + 2 + 3 + ... + 100$

$= (1 + 100) + (2 + 99) + ... + (50 + 51)$ [50 pairs each equal to 101].

This book is an attempt to make clear the basic fundamental concepts which you always wanted to know. It has been designed for students in the age group of 10-18 years who are inquistive by nature and want to understand and master the basic reasoning of every *why* and *how* in mathematics.

I am sure students will love this book as it is certainly going to resolve every doubt in their minds. The language used is very simple, and the logic and explanations are easy to understand. I do hope people from my fraternity too will find this book very useful.

Suggestions to improve the book will be appreciated.

—Rajesh Kr. Thakur
rkthakur1974@gmail.com

CONTENTS

Q. 16 : What is a Binary Numeral system? How are different operations performed in Binary Numeral system?

Q. 17 : How are big numbers written in Roman Numeral system?

Q. 18 : Why is $\pi = \frac{22}{7}$ as taken most of the time?

Q. 19 : Why are scientists finding more and more values of π?

Q. 20 : Why is 22.48 read as twenty two decimal four eight?

Q. 21 : Why $a^{-1} = 1/a$?

Q. 22 : Why $-(-5) = 5$?

Q. 23 : Why is $|-5| = 5$?

Q. 24 : What is special about the number 1729?

Q. 25 : Ramanujan called numbers his personal friends. Are numbers really friends?

Q. 26 : Natural number is represented by 'N', Whole number is represented by 'W', but the set of Integers is represented by 'Z', why?

Q. 7 : What do the words 'Characteristics' and 'Mantissa' mean in Logarithm.

Q. 28 : What is the rule for finding Characteristics?

Q. 29 : How can Mantissa be found?

Q. 30 : What is the use of Logarithm?

Q. 31 : What is Rationalising process?

Q. 32 : Is 13 an inauspicious number in Mathematics too?

Q. 33 : What is a Perfect Number?

Q. 34 : What is special about Fibonacci Number?

Q. 35 : What is a Partition Number?

Q. 36 : What is a Golden Number?

Q. 37 : What is a Beast number?

Q. 38 : What is a Complex Number? Is complex number useful in our daily life?

Q. 39 : How can I know whether a decimal expansion is a terminating or non–terminating decimal?

Q. 40 : In simplification of arithmetical calculation, VBODMAS rule is sometimes followed. Here 'O' and 'M' used for 'of' and 'Multiplication' have the same meaning *i.e.* multiplication. Why are the two letters 'O' and 'M' used instead of the single letter 'M' in VBODMAS rule?

Q. 41 : How did the primitive people count?

Q. 42 : What are the different rules to check the divisibility of a number?

Q. 43 : Is there any rule to check the divisibility of a number by 7?

Q. 44 : What is Casting Out nines method?

Q. 45 : Can animals count?

Q. 46 : How to find the rational numbers between two numbers?

Q. 47 : Can numbers be categorised on the basis of the name of mathematicians?

Q. 48 : What is the rule to find prime between two numbers?

Q. 1 : What is Geometry? What are its different types?

Q. 2 : What do you mean by a polygon?

Q. 3 : What is the difference between convex and concave polygon?

Q. 4 : Define angles. What are its different types?

Q. 5 : What is the difference between centroid, incentre, orthocentre and circumcentre?

Q. 6 : Is the sum of angles of a triangle always equal to 180° ?

Q. 7 : Is there any number which exhibits the geometrical shape in Mathematics?

Q. 8 : What is a quadrilateral? Discuss its different types.

Q. 9 : What does QED and CPCT stand for?

Q. 10 : What is the difference between Polygon and Polyhedron?

Q. 11 : What is the difference between parallelogram and parallelepiped?

Q. 12 : Why does the angle of circle measure 360°?

Q. 13 : How to decide the angle sum of a polygon?

Q. 14 : What is the formula to find the number of diagonals of a polygon?

Q. 15 : What is Nine-point Circles?

Q. 16 : Why do we have 60 seconds in a minute?

Q. 17 : Is circle a polygon?

Q. 18 : What is circumference? How can the circumference of a circle be worked out?

Q. 19 : Let AB be a line segment. Why do we take the arc

length as half or more than half while bisecting the line segment into two equal halves?

Q. 20 : What is the origin of degree?

Q. 21 : For the point P (x_1, y_1) and Q (x_2, y_2) why is the distance between $PQ = \sqrt{(x_2 - x_1)^2 + (y_2 - y_1)^2}$

Q. 22 : For the triangle ABC, with vertex A $(x_1 y_1)$, B (x_2, y_2) and C (x_3, y_3), why is the area of triangle ABC

$$\frac{1}{2}[x_1(y_2 - y_3) + x_2(y_3 - y_1) + x_3(y_1 - y_2)]$$

Q. 23 : What is the origin of word 'Geometry'.

Q. 24 : Can Geometry be related to Nature?

● ALGEBRA 105

Q. 1 : For the given quadratic equation

$ax^2 + bx + c = 0$, why $x = \dfrac{-b \pm \sqrt{b^2 - 4ac}}{2a}$?

Q. 2 : Why $\log_{a^{mn}} = \log_{a^m} + \log_{a^n}$?

Q. 3 : Why $\log a^{m/n} = \log a^m - \log a^n$?

Q. 4 : Why $\log a^1 = 0$?

Q. 5 : Why $\log a^a = 1$?

Q. 6 : Why $a^{\log a^N} = N$?

Q. 7 : Why $n_{P_r} = \dfrac{n!}{n - r!}$ for $0 \le r \le n$?

Q. 8 : Why $^{n}c_{r} = \frac{n!}{r!\,n-r!}$

Q. 9 : What is the difference between Common Logarithm and Natural Logarithm?

Q. 10 : What is the difference between AP, GP and HP?

Q. 11 : Why in an AP, $a_n = a + (n-1)\,d$ where a, d have the same meaning?

Q. 12 : Why $S_n = \frac{n}{2}\{2a + (n-1)d\}$ where a, d have the usual meaning?

Q. 13 : Why $1^2 + 2^2 + 3^2 + \ldots + n^2 = \frac{n(n+1)(2n+1)}{6}$?

Q. 14 : How can general algebraic identities be derived?

Q. 15 : Is zero a multiple of every number ?

Q. 16 : Why

$$1^3 + 2^3 + \ldots\ldots\ldots + n^3 = \frac{n^2(n+1)^2}{4} = \left(\frac{n\,(n+1)}{2}\right)^2 = (\Sigma n)^2 ?$$

Q. 17 : Why $1+2+3+\ldots\ldots\ldots + n = \frac{n(n+1)}{2}$?

Q. 18 : What do you mean by infinity in Mathematics?

Q. 19 : Which one is larger n^n or $(n+1)^{n-1}$?

Q. 20 : If $a > b$ then why $-a < -b$?

Q. 21 : How to add and subtract two inequalilies, say $a > b$ and $c < d$?

Q. 22 : Why $(-a) \times (+b) = -ab$?

Q. 23 : Why $(-a)^{\circ} = 1$ but $-a^{\circ} = -1$?

Q. 24 : Why $\frac{a}{b} = \frac{c}{d} \Rightarrow ad = bc$?

Q. 25 : What is a Golden Triangle?

Q. 26 : What is a Googol?

Q. 27 : What is a Googolplex?

Q. 28 : What is the difference between Monomial, Binomial and Polynomial?

Q. 29 : What is HCF, LCM and LCD?

Q. 30 : Prove product of two numbers = HCF × LCM.

Q. 31 : Prove $n_{c_r} + n_{c_{r-1}} = n + 1_{c_r}$.

Q. 32 : If $n_{c_x} = n_{c_y} \Rightarrow x = y$ or $x + y = n$ Why?

Q. 33 : Prove for $0 \le r \le n, n_{c_r} = nc_{n-r}$

Q. 34 : Solve $\sqrt{x} + y = 11$ and $\sqrt{y} + x = 7$.

Q. 35 : The square root of 16 is 4 *i.e.* $\sqrt{16} = 4$ and 16>4

but $\sqrt{0.16} = 0.4$ and $0.16 < 0.4$. Why?

Q. 36 : Name the mathematicians who have contributed in developing the mathematical symbols?

Q. 37 : Why do we take carry from the preceding digit of minuend when the digit at the same place in subtrahend is greater than that of minuend?

Q. 38 : Why do we put cross mark after each step of multiplication?

Q. 39 : Find the three roots of $\sqrt[3]{1}$.

Q. 40 : In the division process, why is sometimes zero put in the middle quotient to carry down the next number from dividend and in some cases, it is put at the end to finish the division process?

Q. 41 : In dividing a fraction, why

$$\frac{a}{b} \div \frac{c}{d} = \frac{a}{b} \times \frac{d}{c}?$$

Q. 42 : Why $0 \leq P(A) \leq 1$ *i.e.* probability of a number lies between 0 and 1?

Q. 43 : A rectangle has a side 3 m and another 4 m. Is its area 12 metres squared or 12 square metres?

● OTHER FIELDS 143

Q. 1 : What is the oldest mathematical puzzle?

Q. 2 : How can I tell the day of the year?

Q. 3 : What is the highest prize in the field of mathematics?

Q. 4 : Why is there no Nobel prize in Mathematics?

Q. 5 : Are there any mathematicians who have been awarded the Nobel prize in other fields?

Q. 6 : What does Trigonometry mean?

Q. 7 : If B and Q are the acute angles such that Sin B = Sin Q, then why B = Q?

Q. 8 : Prove the following result :

$$\sin^2\theta + \cos^2\theta = 1, \sec^2\theta - \tan^2\theta = 1$$

NUMBER THEORY

Q 1. : Define number and its different types?

Ans. : A number is an idea which answers the question "How many objects in a collection?"

TYPES OF NUMBERS

We can categorise numbers into ten different sections :

(i) Natural Numbers : They are the counting numbers which we learn as a child.

Example : {1, 2, 3, 4, 5,..................}

The set of Natural numbers is denoted by N. This set is infinite. It begins with 1 and the next number is obtained by adding 1 to it. The sum of n natural numbers is given by

$$1 + 2 + 3 + \ldots\ldots\ldots\ldots + n = \frac{n(n+1)}{2}$$

Suppose, you need to find the sum of 20 natural numbers.

i.e. $1 + 2 + 3 + 4 + \ldots\ldots\ldots + 20$

Here $n = 20, n + 1 = 20 + 1 = 21$

$$\text{Hence } \sum_{i=1}^{20} n = \frac{20 \times 21}{2} = 210$$

(ii) Whole Numbers : It is the set of numbers which include 0 and counting numbers. It is denoted by W.

W = {0, 1, 2, 3, ...}

The first whole number is 0 and the set W has infinite numbers.

(iii) Even Numbers : An integer that is divisible by 2 is called an even number.

Example : {0, 2, 4, 6, 8.................}

Many mathematicians do not include 0 in the set of even numbers, but many others are of the opinion that 0 should be included in the set of Even numbers. I am also optimisitic and think that 0 should be included in the set of even numbers.

All even numbers can be written in the form of 2n, where n is any integer.

(iv) Odd Numbers : An integer that is not evenly divisible by 2 is called an odd number. It can be expressed in the form of 2n + 1 where n is any integer.

Example : {1, 3, 5, 7, 9.................}

The sum of n odd number is equal to n^2

i.e. $1 + 3 + 5 + \ldots\ldots\ldots + n = n^2$

(v) Integers : All counting numbers, together with their negatives and zero constitute the set of Integers.

Examples : {...............–5, 4, –3, –2, –1, 0, 1, 2, 3............}

(vi) Rational Numbers : The number of the form of $\frac{p}{q}$ where p and q are integers and $q \neq 0$, is called rational number. It is denoted by Q.

$$Q = \left(\frac{a}{b} : a, b \in Z \text{ and } b \neq 0\right)$$

Every integer is a rational number because each integer (m) can be written as $\frac{m}{1}$.

The set of Rational numbers includes $2, -2, \frac{4}{7}, 0, \frac{7}{4}$ ... etc.

There are infinite rational numbers between any two rational numbers.

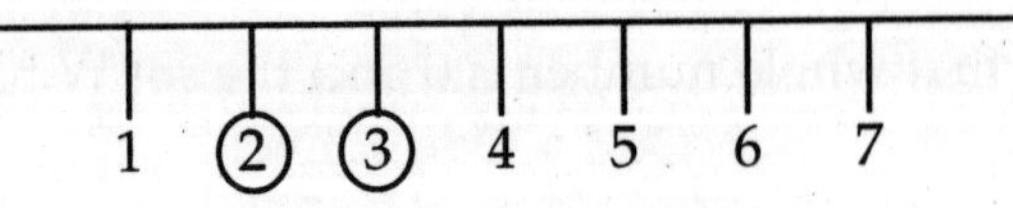

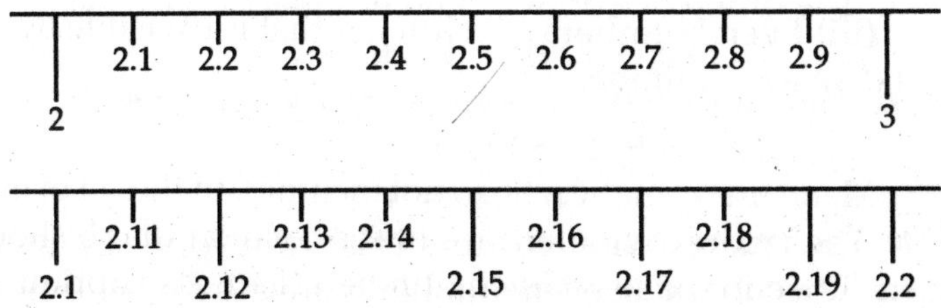

From the above diagram, it is clear that between two rational numbers 2 and 3, there exist infinite rational numbers.

(vii) Irrational Numbers : Any real number that is not rational is called irrational number. In simple terms we can say that a real number not expressible as an integer or quotient of integers is irrational.

Example : $\sqrt{2}, \sqrt{3}, \sqrt{5}, \ldots\ldots\ldots\ldots$

Pythagoras was the first to talk about irrational numbers.

(viii) Real Numbers : The set of rational and irrational numbers is the set of real numbers. It is denoted by R.

Example : $\left\{\ldots\sqrt{2}, 2, -1, 0, \frac{3}{4}\ldots\right\}$

(ix) Complex Numbers : Any number real or imaginary, in the form of a+ib is called complex number.

Example : 2+3i, –3+4i, –4 –5i, etc.

The 'i' is called ***iota*** and is equal to $\sqrt{-1}$.

(x) Prime Numbers : An integer p which is not 0 or ± 1 and is divisible by no integer except ± 1 and itself is called prime number.

Example : 2, 3, 5, 7, 11, 13, 17, 19, 23, etc.

Q.2. : Write the characteristics of even numbers.

Ans : a. The sum of two even numbers is also even, *i.e.*

Even + Even = Even

b. The sum of two odd numbers is an even number, *i.e.*

Odd + Odd = Even

c. The difference of two even numbers is also even.

i.e. Even – Even = Even

d. The product of two even numbers is also even.

Even × Even = Even

e. 2 + 4 + 6 + ... n term = $n^2 + n$

f. The square of an even number is always divisible by 4.

g. The cube of an even number is always divisible by 8.

h. $n_{c_2} + n_{c_4} + n_{c_6} + ... = 2^{n-1} - 1$

Q. 3 : Is 0 an even number?

Ans. Yes, 0 is obviously an even number. An integer that is divisible by 2 or can be written in the form of 2n, where n is an integer, is called an even number.

Here, 0 = 2 × 0

Hence, in accordance with the above property, 0 can be said to be an even number.

In other ways, we know that the sum of two even numbers is even.

Even + Even = Even

Since 2 is even : So is –2

Now as per the above properties.

2 + (–2) = 0

This clearly indicates that 0 is an even number.

Q. 4 : Why does counting begin with 1?

Ans. Primitive men used sign language to indicate numbers. The use of fingers came later. The first journey of numbers began with 'Quipu'. The Quipu was a kind of knot of a rope used earlier to count the herd of sheep and other things.

You will be surprised to know that 1 was not considered as a number till the 15th century. But thanks to Stevin a Flemish mathematician, who dared to consider 1 as a number.

Now, let us return to the question. The best way of counting is by making a mark for the thing counted. Suppose you have seven eggs, then you will write ///////. Similarly for five eggs, you write /////; but if you have no eggs then what will you keep track of?

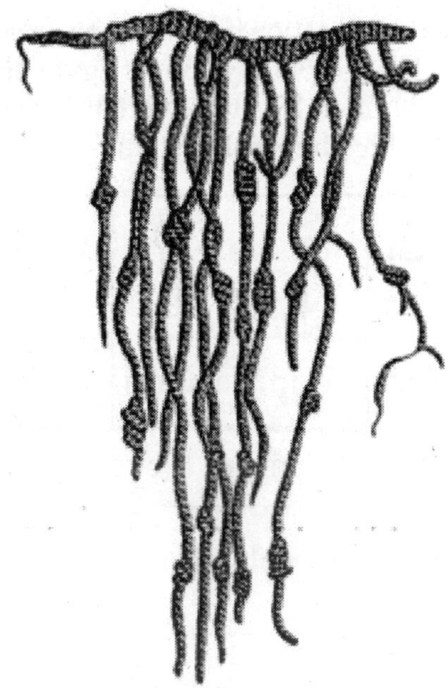

Quipu

The above explanation is enough to tell you why counting begins with 1 and not with zero.

Q. 5. Write the characteristics of odd number.

a. The sum of two odd numbers is even

i.e. Odd + Odd = Even

b. The difference of two odd numbers is even.

Odd – Odd = Even

c. The sum of n odd numbers is n^2

$1 + 3 + 5 + \ldots\ldots\ldots + n = n^2$

d. The product of an even number and an odd number is even.

Even × odd = Even

e. $n_{c_1} + n_{c_3} + n_{c_5} + \ldots\ldots\ldots$upto n terms $= 2^n - 1$

f. The square of an odd number is in the form of 4n + 1.

Q. 6. What were the different numeral systems used earlier?

Before the acceptance of Hindu–Arabic Numeral System

used today, every civilisation had their own system of writing numerals. The Hieroglyphic System of Egypt, the Babylonian and the Roman Numeral System were the most familar.

a. Hieroglyphic Numeral System

1	10	100	1000	10000	100000	10^6

Egyptian numeral hieroglyphs

b. Babylonian Numeral System

1	11
2	12
3	13
4	14
5	15
6	16
7	17
8	18
9	19
10	20

c. Roman Numeral System

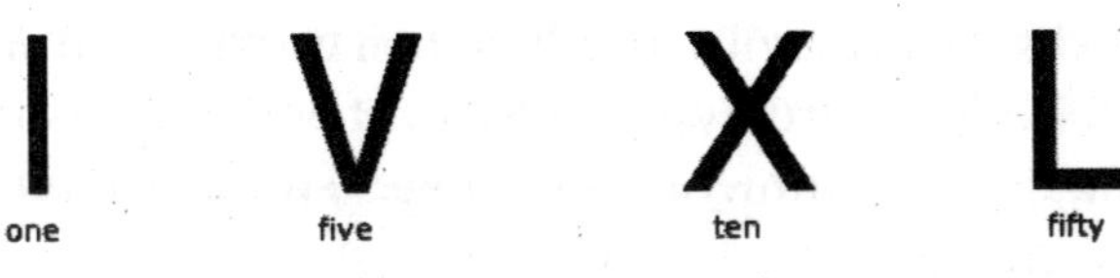

C D M

one hundred five hundred one thousand

d. Hindu–Arabic Numerals

Brahmi		—	=	≡	+	[illegible]	[illegible]	[illegible]	[illegible]	[illegible]
Hindu	०	१	२	३	४	५	६	७	८	९
Arabic	٠	١	٢	٣	٤	٥	٦	٧	٨	٩
Medieval	o	I	2	3	[illegible]	[illegible]	6	ʌ	8	9
Modern	0	1	2	3	4	5	6	7	8	9

Except the Mayan Numeral system, no other system had a different symbol for zero. The introduction of zero by Hindu mathematician brought a revolutionary change in writing the larger numbers without much difficulty.

Q. 6 : Who introduced zero?

Ans : Let me begin the journey of zero with the famous line of G.B. Halsted.

"The importance of the creation of the zero mark can never be exaggerated. This which gives us airy nothing not merely a local habitation, name, a picture, a symbol but helpful power, is the characteristic of the Hindu race from when a it spiang. It is like coining the NIRVANA into dynamos. No single mathematical creation has been more potent for the general on-go of intelligence and power."

There is no doubt that zero was an Indian creation. The

earliest known reference to zero seems to appear in Acharya Pingla's book *Chanda–sastra*, where he writes.

गायत्रे षड़संख्यामर्धेडपनीते द्वयडके अवशिष्ट स्त्रयस्तेषु
रूपमपनीय द्वयडकायः शून्यं स्थापत्यम्॥

i.e. In Gayatri Chanda one pada has 6 letters, when the number is made half it becomes three. Remove one from it and make it half to get 1. Remove 1 from it thus get the zero.

In Mathematical terms :

$$\frac{1}{2}\times\left\{\frac{1}{2}\times 6-1\right\}-1=0$$

Varahamihir (505–589 AD) in his famous book. *Panchasiddhanta* written in 575 AD had many a times used the place–value system, containing zero which is believed to be fairly proven for the use of zero for the first time.

Brahmagupta in his book *Brahma–Sputa–Siddhanta* defined the operation of zero for the first time, where he writes a – a = 0

Q. 7 : What are the unique properties of zero?

Ans. : The unique properties of zero are :

a. 0 is the additive identity

i.e. any number + zero = the number itself a + 0 = a

b. When zero is placed to the right of 1, the number becomes ten. By continuing to put zero to the right of 1, we make the value of 1 ten times greater.

1 = 1

10 = 1 × 10 = Ten

100 = 10 × 10 = Hundred

1000 = 10 × 100 = Thousand

10000 = 10 ×1000 = Ten Thousand

c. If zero is put to the left of 1 with a decimal point before it, the value becomes one-tenth. Two zeros make it one-hundredth. Three zeros make it one-thousandth and so on.

$$0.1 = \frac{1}{10} \text{ One} - \text{tenth.}$$

$$0.01 = \frac{1}{100} = \frac{1}{10} \times \frac{1}{10} = \text{One} - \text{hundredth}$$

$$0.001 = \frac{1}{1000} = \frac{1}{10} \times \frac{1}{100} = \text{One} - \text{thousandth}$$

d. Any number, except zero, multiplied by zero is always zero.

$$a \times 0 = a$$

e. Any number, except zero, divided by zero is undefined.

$$\frac{a}{0} = \infty \text{ (undefined)}$$

f. Zero divided by any number, except zero is zero.

$$\frac{0}{a} = 0$$

g. Power zero to any number is one.

$$a^0 = 1$$

h. The factorial of zero is also 1.

$$0! = 1$$

Q. 9 : Why $a^0 = 1$?

Ans : This sounds absurd that power of zero to any number is one, but this is a truth. Let me remind you of the rule of indices.

$$a^{m-n} = \frac{a^m}{a^n}$$

You can prove this rule by a simple example. Suppose you have to divide x^5 by x^2.

i.e. $x^5 \div x^2 = ?$

Now $x^5 = x \times x \times x \times x \times x$

and $x^2 = x \times x$

Hence, $\frac{x^5}{x^2} = \frac{x \times x \times x \times x \times x}{x \times x} = x^3$

This can be easily understood with the help of the generalised formulae for equal base, written above.

Now, consider a case, when m = n

$$a^{m-n} = \frac{a^m}{a^n}$$

For m = n

$$LHS = a^{m-n} = a^{m-m} = a^0$$

$$RHS = \frac{a^m}{a^n} = \frac{a^m}{a^m} = 1$$

Hence $a^0 = 1$?

Q. 10 : Why 0! = 1

Ans : Here ! is called the factorial in mathematical language. The factorial is also written by (L) sign.

What does factorial of a number say ?

The factorial of a number is the product of that number to every other predecessor till 1.

In other words.

6! = 6 × 5 × 4 × 3 × 2 × 1 = 720

5! = 5 × 4 × 3 × 2 × 1= 120

4! = 4 × 3 × 2 × 1 = 24

3! = 3 × 2 × 1 = 6

2! = 2 × 1 = 2

1! = 1

Now, let us return to the proof.

We know

$$n_{P_n} = n!$$

Let us take the case of arranging 'r' objects out of n objects. *i.e.* n_{P_r}

$$n_{p_r} = \frac{n!}{n-r!}$$

If n = r

$$n_{p_n} = \frac{n!}{n-n!}$$

As stated above $n_{p_n} = n!$

$$\Rightarrow \frac{n!}{1} = \frac{n!}{0!}$$

n! × 0! = n! (By cross multiplication)

$$\Rightarrow 0! = \frac{n!}{n!} = 1$$

Q. 11 : Why $\frac{1}{0}$ is undefined?

Ans : Division is a process of repeated subtraction.

Example : Divide 16 by 2.

Solution : We know 16 ÷ 2 = 8

Now, let us understand this basic concept of division by means of repeated subtraction.

16 ÷ 2 = ?

16 – 2	= 14	1st stage
14 – 2	= 12	2nd stage
12 – 2	= 10	3rd stage
10 – 2	= 8	4th stage
8 – 2	= 6	5th stage
6 – 2	= 4	6th stage
4 – 2	= 2	7th stage
2 – 2	= 0	8th stage

From the above explanation, it is clear that the final remainder '0' can be reached after 8th stage. Hence 16 ÷ 2 = 8

Now let us return to our original problem.

1 ÷ 0 = ?

Understand this with repeated subtraction method :

$\begin{array}{r} 1 \\ -0 \\ \hline 1 \end{array}$	$\begin{array}{r} 1 \\ -0 \\ \hline 1 \end{array}$	$\begin{array}{r} 1 \\ -0 \\ \hline 1 \end{array}$	$\begin{array}{r} 1 \\ -0 \\ \hline 1 \end{array}$
1st stage	2nd stage	3rd stage	4th stage

So, you can't get the final remainder 0 whatsoever attempts you make.

Hence $\frac{1}{0}$ = undefined

Let us understand it in another way – division is the inverse operation to multiplication.

$$\frac{6}{2}=3$$
$$\Rightarrow 2\times 3=6$$

In other words, if the quotient $\frac{a}{b}$ of two numbers a and b is c, then b × c = a

Suppose, $\frac{1}{0}=x$

$$\Rightarrow x\times 0=1$$

But the product of any number with zero can never give the result 1. Since there is no such number which can fit in the above situation, so mathematicians have agreed upon a word 'undefined' for such a situation

Hence $\frac{1}{0}$ = undefined.

Q. 12 : Why $\frac{0}{0} \neq 1$.

Ans : There is a very interesting story about 0 ÷ 0.

A teacher once said, "Any number divided by itself gives the quotient 1"

Ramanujan, a class III student then, asked, "Sir, what about 0 divided by 0"?

The teacher scolded Ramanujan for having asked such, stupid question.

It is a well established fact that any number divided by itself gives 1 as a quotient.

$1 \div 1 = 1$ $\quad$ $10 \div 10 = 1$

$1000 \div 1000 = 1$ ....etc.

This would certainly make $0 \div 0 = 1$.

Moreover, if we reverse the process we find that $1 \times 0 = 0$, which again gives the strong case to believe us that $\frac{0}{0} = 1$. But let us think this broadly.

There is another established fact in mathematics.

Any number $\times\, 0 = 0$

Hence

$1 \times 0 = 0$ $\quad$ $2 \times 0 = 0$

$3 \times 0 = 0$ $\quad$ $4 \times 0 = 0$

$1000000 \times 0 = 0$ $\quad$ $10000000000 \times 0 = 0$

So, if we divide $\frac{0}{0}$ in all the above taken cases we will have the different quotient all together.

Henceforth, we call $\frac{0}{0}$ an **indeterminate form.**

Q. 13 : Why is 1 not a prime number?

Ans : A number is said to be prime, if it had two factors 1 and the number itself. But 1 has a unique feature. It can be written in so many ways :

$$1 = 1 \times 1$$
$$= 1 \times 1 \times 1$$
$$= 1 \times 1 \times 1 \times 1$$

Now, let us learn some other things about prime numbers.

- Two numbers are said to be co–prime, if their H.C.F. (Highest Common Factor) is 1. Co–primes are not necessarily

Primes. For example, 8 and 9 are co–primes but none of them is a prime number.

● A pair of Prime Numbers is said to be Twin Prime Pair if the two numbers differ by 2. Example : (3, 5), (5, 7), (11, 13), (17, 19), (29, 31), (41, 43), (59, 61), (71, 73) etc.

● 2 is the largest Even prime number.

● 3 is the smallest Odd prime number.

● Every even integer greater than 2 can be expressed as the sum of two prime numbers.

Example : $8 = 3 + 5$

$16 = 13 + 3$

$60 = 13 + 47$

The above properties is called Goldbach's conjecture.

● Every even integer greater than 4 can be written as the sum of two odd prime numbers.

$4 = 2 + 2$

$= 1 + 3$

$6 = 3 + 3$

$= 1 + 5$

Q. 14 : Why is 0.99 considered equivalent to 1?

Ans : This can be better understood in two ways :

a. By the concept of Real Numbers

b. Using the concept of Geometric Series.

By the concept of Real Numbers :

Let us assume, x = 0.999.......... (1)

Multiply the equation (1) by 10

10x = 9.99.................................... (2)

Subtract (1) from (2), we get,

10x – x = 9.99 – 0.99 (7)....................

$\Rightarrow 9x = 9$

$\Rightarrow x = \frac{9}{9} = 1$

If you are familar with the Geometric Progression series, you can understand the whole concept in a line. Let me first tell you what a G.P. is?

G.P. is the abbreviation used for Geometric Progression It is a sequence for which the ratio of a term to its predecessor is the same for all terms.

The general form of a G.P. is

$a, ar, ar^2, ar^3 \ldots\ldots\ldots ar^{n-1}$

Where a is the first term and r is the common ratio and ar^{n-1} is the last (n^{th}) term of a finite Geometric sequence.

Example : 1, 2, 4, 8, 16, 32, 64.............

b. 2, 8, 32.....................

In a G.P. for infinite sequence, the sum of a number is given by a/1–r *i.e.*

$$a + ar + ar^2 + \ldots = \frac{a}{1-r}$$

Now, Let us return to the question.

$0.999\ldots = 0.9 + 0.09 + 0.009 + \ldots\ldots\ldots$

$$= \frac{9}{10} + \frac{9}{100} + \frac{9}{1000} + \ldots$$

$$= 9\left(\frac{1}{10} + \frac{1}{10^2} + \frac{1}{10^3} + \ldots\right)$$

This is clearly a G.P. for infinite sequence. Hence, we shall apply the above formulae.

$$S_\infty = \frac{a}{1-r}$$

$$= 9 \times \left(\frac{\frac{1}{10}}{1-\frac{1}{10}}\right)$$

$$= \cancel{9} \times \frac{1}{\cancel{10}} \times \frac{\cancel{10}}{\cancel{9}} = 1$$

Q. 15 : What is the rounding off system used in mathematics?

Ans : It is a common practice to keep one or two digits

after decimal and leave the remaining. Dropping decimals after a certain significant place is termed as Rounding off system in mathematics.

Example :

2.387 can be rounded off to 2.39 or 2.4

Rules :

a. When the first digit dropped is less than 5, the preceeding digit isn't changed.

Example : 2.43 is rounded off to 2.4

b. When the first digit dropped is 5 or greater than 5, and some succeeding digit is not zero, the preceding digit is increased by 1.

Example :

2.58 is rounded off to 2.6

c. When the first digit dropped is 5, and all the succeeding digits are zero, the commonly accepted rule is to make the preceding digit even, *i.e.* add 1 to it if it is odd and leave it alone if it is already even.

Example : 2.324, 2.316 and 2.3

(i) 2.4005 is rounded off to three places to write 2.4

(ii) 2.3005 is also rounded off to 2.4

Q. 16 : What is Binary Numeral system? How are different operations performed in Binary Numeral system?

Ans : A system of numerals for representing real numbers that has the base 2 instead of base 10 is called binary numeral system.

There are only two symbols 0 and 1 used for Binary numeral system.

CHARACTERISTICS OF BINARY NUMBER SYSTEM

- It is used in computers.
- In base two, odd numbers always end in 1 while even numbers end in 0.
- A binary number gets doubled if an extra zero is placed after the number.

Example : 100110 = 2 × 10011

HOW IS A BINARY NUMBER EXPRESSED?

A binary number is expressed by writing 'two' at the bottom of the number.

Example : In binary system, 1 is written as $(1)_2$

DIFFERENT OPERATIONS IN BINARY SYSTEM

Let us first see how a decimal number is changed into binary system.

Example : Change $(102)_{10}$ into binary system.

Solution :

2	102	Remainder
2	51	0
2	25	1
2	12	1
2	6	0
2	3	0
	1	1

Hence, $(102)_{10} = (1100110)_2$

Addition :

$$\begin{array}{r} 11010 \\ +10111 \\ \hline 110001 \\ \hline \end{array}$$

Explanation : 0 + 1 = 0 is one's place

1 + 1 = 10, Write 0 in second place.

and so on

2 in decimal expansion = 10 in binary

3 in decimal expansion = 11 in binary

Subtraction :

$$\begin{array}{r} 110 \\ -101 \\ \hline 1 \\ \hline \end{array}$$

Explanation : We cannot subtract 1 from 0 at one's place so, we take 1 unit from the next position and consider it 2 as we take 10 as carrying from the preceding ten's. Hence write 1 at the one's place. The next operation is 0 – 0 = 0 and 1 –1=0

Multiplication :

$$\begin{array}{r} 10 \\ \times\ 11 \\ \hline 10 \\ 10\times \\ \hline 110 \\ \hline \end{array}$$

Explanation : 1 × 0 = 0 and 1 × 1 = 1

The rest of the process is same as in general multiplication.

Q. 17 : How are big numbers written in Roman Numeral system written?

Ans : A system of writing numeral integers used by the Romans is known as Roman Numeral System. The Roman system of numbers was probably derived from Etruscans, the earlier inhabitants of Italy. Letters were used for numerals.

The integers from 1 to 10 in Roman Numerals :

I	=	1	II	=	2
III	=	3	IV	=	4
V	=	5	VI	=	6
VII	=	7	VIII	=	8
IX	=	9	X	=	10

Let us learn the rules of writing an integer in Roman Numeral system.

a. When a letter is repeated or immediately followed by a letter of lesser value, the values are added.

II = 2 III = 3

b. When a letter is immediately followed by a letter of greater value, the smaller is subtracted from the larger.

IX = 9 XL = 40

c. The symbol I can be subtracted from V and X only.

d. The symbol X can be subtracted from L, M and C only.

e. If a symbol is repeated, its value is added as many times as it occurs.

XX = 20 CC = 100

f. A symbol is not repeated more than three times but V, L and D are never repeated.

g. The symbol V, L and D are never written to the left of a symbol of greater value.

ROMAN NUMERAL CHART

Roman Numeral Table			
1 I	14 XIV	27 XXVII	150 CL
2 II	15 XV	28 XXVIII	200 CC
3 III	16 XVI	29 XXIX	300 CCC
4 IV	17 XVII	30 XXX	400 CD
5 V	18 XVIII	31 XXXI	500 D
6 VI	19 XIX	40 XL	600 DC
7 VII	20 XX	50 L	700 DCC
8 VIII	21 XXI	60 LX	800 DCCC
9 IX	22 XXII	70 LXX	900 CM
10 X	23 XXIII	80 LXXX	1000 M
11 XI	24 XXIV	90 XC	1600 MDC
12 XII	25 XXV	100 C	1700 MDCC
13 XIII	26 XXVI	101 CI	1900 MCM

Q. 18 : Why is π taken as $\frac{22}{7}$ most of the time?

Ans : We all know that π (Pi) is the ratio of circumference to diameter.

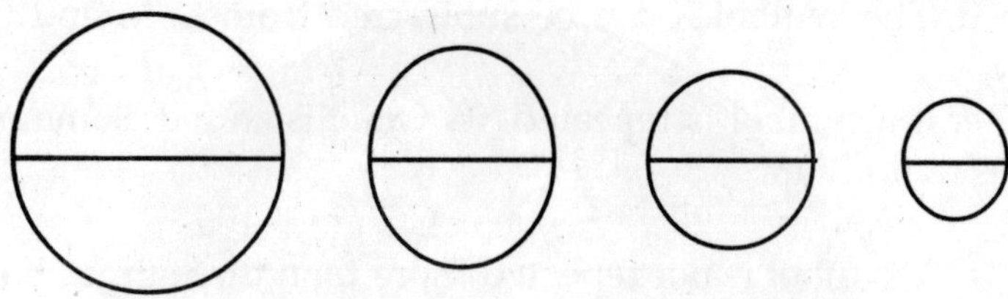

However big the circle, the ratio of its circumference to its diameter is a constant and that constant is called π (pi).

Archimedes is considered by some western mathematicians to be the first to give the value of π, but even Archimedes had a rough idea as he took π in between $\frac{22}{7}$ and $\frac{223}{71}$. To prove this Archimedes inscribed and circumscribed regular polygons of 96 sides and showed that the upper limit is $\frac{22}{7}$ and the lower limit is $\frac{223}{71}$. Archimedes probably knew what so many people today don't know that pi is not equal to $\frac{22}{7}$ and made no claim to have discovered the exact value of π. I do think probably all mathematicians had agreed upon to pay a great honour to the genius Archimedes and began to consider π is somehow equivalent to $\frac{22}{7}$.

You will be astonished to know that if we take the best estimate as the average of the two bounds $\frac{22}{7}$ and $\frac{223}{71}$ discovered by Archimedes we obtain 3.1418, *i.e.* an error of 0.0002 to the value of π upto four decimal places :

Archimedes is considered by some western mathematicians to be the first to give...

Q. 19 : Why are scientists finding more and more values of π ?

Ans : Mathematicians all over the world seem to be crazy to find the more and more values of pi. With the emergence of computer, this craziness crossed the limit. In 1966 the value of π, correct to 25000 places after decimal, was found by using IBM and a milestone was achieved in Paris when the labour of 28 hours 10 miniutes on CDC 6600 helped the mathematicians to find the value of π up to 500000 places after decimal.

The craze of finding more and more value of π seems useless and it is interesting here to tell you that in 1755 the French Academy of Science declined to examine any more value of π.

Now the big question is — why are scientists crazy about pi? Is there any use to find such large values?

In Hermann–Schubert's view–"*Conceive a sphere constructed with the earth as its centre, and imagine its surface to pass through Sirius, which is 8.8 light years distant from the earth then imagine this enormous sphere to be so packed with microbes that in every cubic millimetre millions of millions of these diminutive animalcula are present. Now conceive these microbes to be unpacked and so distributed singly along a straight line that every two microbes are as far distant from each other as Sirius from us, i.e. 8.8 light years. Conceive this long line thus fixed by all the microbes as the diameter of a circle, and imagine the circumference of it to be calculated by multiplying its diometer by π to 100 decimal places. Then, in the case of a circle of this enormous magnitude even, the circumference so calculated would not vary from the real circumference by a millionth part of a millimetre."*

This example shows that there is no need to calculate 100, 200 or more value of π. Calculating π to more and more values after decimal is to make our universe understand fully, as pi is fundamental to the way in which our universe functions.

Mathematician Petr Beckmann writes in *A History of* Pi: For the most part, I suspect, that driving force behind these calculations was the spirit that makes people go over Niagara Falls in a barrel or to top the world record of pole sitting by another 20 minutes.

Q. 20 : Why 22.48 is read as twenty-two decimal four eight?

Ans : Every decimal number has two parts :

a. Whole Part

b. Fractional Part

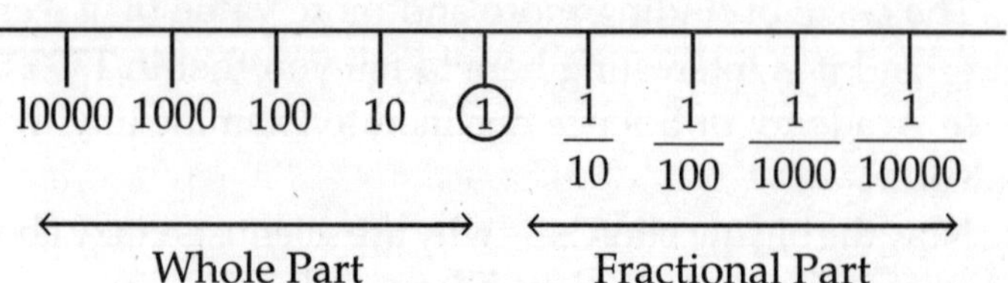

In the given question, 22 is the whole part and 48 is the fractional part. From the above diagram, it is clear that every individual succeeding number in the fractional part is $\frac{1}{10}$th, $\frac{1}{100}$th, $\frac{1}{1000}$th....... of the preceding one.

Now expand 22.48 as follows :

$22.48 = 22 + 0.48$

$= 2 \times 10^1 + 2 + \frac{4}{10} + \frac{8}{100}$

This gives us the better picture that $\frac{4}{10}$ and $\frac{8}{100}$ both numbers placed after decimal are less than 1 and so there is no question to read .48 as forty-eight instead of four eight separately.

Now let us take some more examples.

- 324.709 is read as three hundred twenty four decimal seven zero nine.
- 7.8257 is read as seven decimal eight two five seven.

Q. 21 : Why $x^{-1} = \frac{1}{x}$?

Ans : The law of indices says

$$\frac{x^m}{x^n} = x^{m-n}$$

Consider the case when $n = m + 1$

$$LHS = \frac{x^m}{x^n} = \frac{x^m}{x^{m+1}}$$

$$= \frac{x^m}{x^m . x^1}$$

$$= \frac{1}{x}$$

$RHS = x^{m-n}$

$= x^{m-(m+1)}$

$= x^{m-m-1}$
$= x^{-1}$

Hence $\frac{1}{x} = x^{-1}$

To simplify it more, take m = 0 and n = 1

$$\text{LHS} = \frac{x^m}{x^n} = \frac{x^0}{x^1} = \frac{1}{x^1}$$

$$\text{RHS} = x^{m-n}$$
$$= x^{0-1}$$
$$= x^{-1}$$

Hence $\frac{1}{x} = x^{-1}$

Q. 22 : Why –(–5) = 5 ?

Ans : This seems to be a very confusing concept in algebra : why (–) × (–) = + ?

When I was a student of sixth standard, I had a tough time with such questions in Algebra. I do not know how many times I had been scolded by my father? O.K. leave me with my childhood memories and let me explain the reason to you.

Logic 1 : You must have noticed in your daily life that the image of an object inside the mirror is opposite to the object. If we consider the negative integers as the image of the corresponding positive integers, then we can understand the concept behind it quite easily.

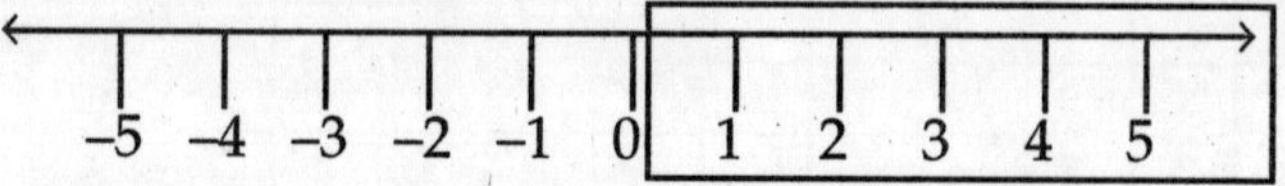

Take a mirror and put it at 0 facing negative integers. The image of –5 is clearly 5. Since we denote the image by negative (–) sign, so –(–5) = 5.

Logic 2 : Let us make a multiplication table.

x	1	2	3	4	5
1	1	2	3	4	5
2	2	4	6	8	10
3	3	6	9	12	15
4	4	8	13	16	20
5	5	10	15	20	25

Did you notice any pattern?

Yes, the above table can be constructed by the process of repeated addition.

For the 1st row, 1 is added to each preceding number to complete the table.

$1 + 1 = 2 \quad 2 + 1 = 3 \quad 3 + 1 = 4$ and $4 + 1 = 5$

For the 2nd row, 2 is added to each preceding number.

$2 + 2 = 4 \quad 4 + 2 = 6 \quad 6 + 2 = 8$ and $8 + 2 = 10$ and so on...

Let us make another multiplication table, but mind one thing that you will have to complete the table by following the above pattern.

Head→ Row	×	+5	+4	+3	+2	+1	0	–1	–2	–3	–4	–5
↓ Head Column	+5	25	20	15	10	5	0	–5	–10	–15	–20	–25
	+4	20	16	12	8	4	0	–4	–8	–12	–16	–20
	+3	15	12	9	6	3	0	–3	–6	–9	–12	–15
	+2	10	8	6	4	2	0	–2	–4	–6	–8	–10
	+1	5	4	3	2	1	0	–1	–2	–3	–4	–5
	0	0	0	0	0	0	0	0	0	0	0	0
	–1	–5	–4	–3	–2	–1	0	1	2	3	4	5
	–2	–10	–8	–6	–4	–2	0	2	4	6	8	10
	–3	–15	–12	–9	–6	–3	0	3	6	9	12	15
	–4	–20	–16	–12	–8	–4	0	4	8	12	16	20
	–5	25	20	15	10	5	0	5	10	15	20	25

The above table has been prepared by following a pattern without using the actual multiplication. The first head row has been written in such a way that every next number followed is 1 less than the previous one.

	$5-1=4$	$4-1=3$	$3-1=2$
$2-1=1$	$1-1=0$	$0-1=-1$	$-1-1=-2$
	$-2-1=-3$	$-3-1=-4$	$-4-1=-5$

The first line of the result is also prepared by following the same pattern. In the first line, every next number is 5 less than the previous one.

$25-5=20$	$20-5=15$	$15-5=10$
$10-5=5$	$5-5=0$	$0-5=-5$
$-5-5=-10$	$-10-5=-15$	$-15-5=-20$
$-20-5=-25$		

Following the same pattern, first complete the whole table. Now, let us check the different results from the given multiplication table.

Case 1 : $(+5) \times (+5) = ?$

See the above table and find out the result in the intersection of +5 in Head Row and + 5 in Head Column. You will reach at 25.

Case 2 : $(+5) \times (-5) = ?$

See the +5 in Head Row and (–5) in Head Column and check the result, where both the row and column coincide. What did you get this time?

This is absolutely –25.

Case 3 : $(-5) \times (-5) = ?$

Look at the point where the (–5) in the Head Row and (–5) in Head column coincides. Did you reach at +25?

Yes, certainly you will have the same answer.

Hence we can conclude $(-) \times (-) = +$

Therefore $-(-5)$ can be written as +5

Q. 23 : Why is $|-5| = 5$

Ans : The modulus (| |) sign denotes the absolute value of an integer.

Let 'a' be any real number then, there is a point on the

number line which corresponds to the number a. The distance of this point from the point 0 is called the **absolute value** of 'a'. Since the distance is always non–negative, the absolute value of a number is always taken positive regardless of the sign of a number.

i.e. $|-5| = 5$

and $|+5| = 5$

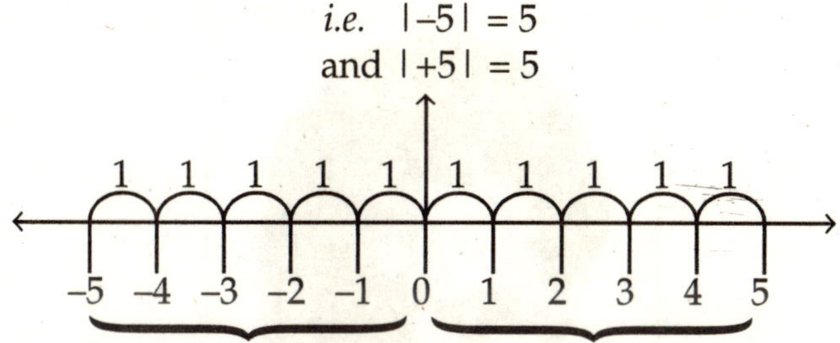

Distance of –5 from 0 = 1 + 1 + 1 + 1 + 1 = 5 unit

Distance of +5 from 0 = 1 + 1 + 1 + 1 + 1 = 5 unit

Q. 24 : What is special about the number 1729?

Ans : 1729 is called the Ramanujan Number. This is the least number which can be easily expressed as the sum of the cubes of two numbers in different ways.

$1729 = 10^3 + 9^3$

$= 12^3 + 1^3$

This was in fact the number of a taxi, Prof. Hardy had hired when he came to see the ailing Ramanujan in the hospital. When Professor Hardy told Ramanujan that the taxi he had hired had a boring number, he instantly replied that this was the smallest number which could be expressed as the sum of cubes of two numbers in two different ways.

Ramanujan was born on December 22, 1887 at Erode in Madras Presidency in a very poor family. He passed his primary education in 1897, scoring first in the district but could not pass his F.A. Prof. Hardy was very much impressed when he got a letter from Ramanujan and invited him to England. He was awarded the B.A. degree and he became the Fellow of Royal Society. Prof. Hardy wrote, "Ramanujan was my discovery. I did not invent him like other great men, he invented himself but I was the first really competent person who had the chance to see some of his work, and still remember with satisfaction that I could recognise at once what treasure I had found."

Ramanujan worked on partition number, hyper geometric series and divergent series.

Srinivasa Ramanujan

Q. 25 : Ramanujan had called numbers his personal friends. Are the numbers really friends?

Ans : Yes, two numbers are friends to each other. There is a special name for such numbers. They are called Amicable numbers.

Amicable Numbers : Two numbers are called Amicable if each is equal to the sum of all the exact divisors of the other except the number itself. 220 and 284 is the first pair of amicable numbers. 220 has the exact divisors 1, 2, 3, 4, 5, 10, 11, 20, 22, 44, 55 and 110 whose sum is 284; and 284 had the exact divisors 1, 2, 4, 71 and 142 whose sum is 220.

$1 + 2 + 3 + 4 + 5 + 10 + 11 + 20 + 22 + 44 + 55 + 110 = 284$

$1+2+4+71+142 = 220$

Another pair of amicable numbers is 1184 and 1210.

There is an unauthentic ated story of that a prince whose name from the standpoint of numerology was equivalent to 284. He sought a bride whose name would represent 220 believing that such combination would guarantee for a happy marriage.

Here are the first ten Amicable Pairs.

Pair	1st	2nd
1	220	284
2	1184	1210
3	2620	2924
4	5020	5564
5	6232	6368
6	10744	10856
7	12285	14595
8	17296	18416
9	63020	76048
10	66928	66992

Q. 26 : Natural number is represented by 'N', whole number is represented by 'W', but the set of Integers is represented by 'Z', why?

Ans : (The definations of natural number, whole number etc. is given in Question No. 1)

Every symbol given to a set of numbers is generally the first letter of the name of the kind of number the set contains. For example : The set of Natural numbers is denoted by **N** (the first letter of Natural). The set of Real numbers is denoted by **R** (the first letter of Real) and so on. Since Integers and Irrational both begin with **I** hence, the mathematician began to look for another symbol to denote the Integers.

In German the word *Zahlen* means to count and *Zahl* means number. Probably the letter **Z** to denote the integers has its origin from these words.

N = {1, 2, 3, 4, 5..............}

$W = \{0, 1, 2, 3, 4..........\}$

$$R = \left\{\frac{-2}{3}, 5, 1, 0, \frac{4}{7}........\right\}$$

$Z = \{-2, -1, 0, 1, 2\}$

Q. 7 : What do the words Characteristics and Mantissa mean in Logarithm.

Ans : The concept of logarithm is based on indices.

If $a^x = N$

$\Rightarrow \log a^N = x$

and $N = \text{antilog } a^x$

Here the operator 'Log' written in front of number means, "look up in the table the power to which 'a' has to be raised to give the number" whereas the operator 'Antilog' means, "Look up in the table the value of the base when raised to the power represented by the number."

Any positive number n in decimal form can be written as :

$n = m \times 10^p$

Where p is any integer and $1 \leq m \leq 10$.

e.g. $55.7 = 5.57 \times 10^1$

$0.00012 = 1.2 \times 10^{-4}$

$1.2 = 1.2 \times 10^0$

If we take log of $n = m \times 10^p$, we have

$\log n = \log m + p \log 10$

$= \log m + p \; [\because \log 10 = 1]$

(Where $1 \leq m \leq 10$)

Clearly, the log of any positive number 'n' consists of two parts.

- The integral part **p** which may be positive, negative or zero.
- The decimal part **log m** that lies between o and 1.

The integral part is called Characteristics and the

decimal part is called the Mantissa. Professor Briggs in 1624 introduced these two words. Always remember that mantissa can never be negative and it will always be less than 1, though characteristics may be positive, negative or zero.

Q. 28 : What is the rule for finding Characteristics?

Ans : There are generally two rules to find characteristics of any given number.

Rule 1 : If the number given is greater than or equal to 1, Characteristics = Number of digits to the left of decimal point – 1

Example : Find the characteristics of 315.4

Solution : Number of digits before decimal = 3

Hence characteristics = 3 – 1 = 2

Example : Find the characteristics of 5.2935?

Solution : Number of digits before decimal = 1

Hence, characteristics = 1 – 1 = 0

Rule 2 : If the given number is less than 1, characteristics = – (Number of zeroes after decimal point, but before the first non zero digit of the number + 1)

Example : Find the characteristics of 0.0001052?

Solution : Number of zeroes after decimal = 3

Characteristics = –(3 + 1) = –4

= –4

Example : Find the characteristics of 0.022438?

Solution : Number of zero after decimal = 1

Characteristics = – (1 + 1)

$= -2 = \bar{2}$

Example : Find the characteristics of 0.0001033?

Solution : Number of zeroes after decimal = 3

Characteristics = – (3+1)

$= -4 = \bar{4}$

Q. 29 : How can Mantissa be found?

Ans : Before the 18th century every logarithmic table had characteristic printed, but from the 18th century onwards the custom of printing only the mantissa became popular.

The log table which use today to find the mantissa consists of 90 rows and 20 columns. Every row begins with the two-digit number 10, 11, 12.........98, 99 and every column is headed by a one-digit number 0 ,1 ,2........9. On the very right of the table there is a big column divided into 9 sub columns 1, 2, 3............9 called the column of mean differences.

											Mean Differences								
N	O	1	2	3	4	5	6	7	8	9	1	2	3	4	5	6	7	8	9
10																			
11																			
12																			
13																			

Note that to find the mantissa of a number we ignore the decimal point of a number and consider the first four digits from the left most side of the number. In case of a number in decimal form, we start calculating the mantissa beginning with first non–zero digit.

ALGORITHM

1. Following the above rule, see the first two digits in column N.
2. In the same row, lock for the column headed by the third digit and if there is no third digit, look the number in the column headed by zero.
3. If there is fourth digit of the given number move in the same row to the column of the mean differences and add this number to the number obtained in the second stage

Example : Find log 2579?

Solution : Characteristics = 4 – 1 = 3

For Mantissa, look the number = 25 in column N and

move to column headed by the third digit 7 to obtain a number 4099. Again move to the same row under the column of mean differences and look for the fourth digit 9 to obtain 15. Add these two. Now our result is 4099 + 15 = 4114

Hence log 2579 = 3.4114

In the same way, log 0.2579 = $\bar{1}$.4114
and log 25.79 = 1.4114

Q. 30 : What is the use of logarithm?

Ans : The use of logarithm is not limited but it has a wide application. The emergence of computer has reduced the usefulness of logarithm table a little but we can hardly ignore the charisma the logarithm play in the common student's life while calculating cumbersome mathematical calculations. Following are the uses of logarithm :

a. In chemical solution, the **ph** of acidity is measured by using the logarithm.
b. To measure the intensity of earthquake on Richter scale.
c. Sound intensity, the brightness of light and many other natural processes are measured on logarithmic scale.
d. In solving the area in calculus.
e. In calculation of compound interest.
f. In calculation of population growth.
g. In calculation of depreciation value.

Q. 31 : What is Rationalising process?

Ans : To remove radicals without altering the value of an expression or the result of an equation is known as Rationalisation.

Case 1 : To rationalise an algebric expression means to remove the radicals which contain the variable (not possible always).

Case 2 : To rationalise the denominator of a fraction means to multiply numerator and denominator by a quantity such that the resulting expression contains no radicals in the denominator.

Example :

Case 1 : Solve $\sqrt{x-1} = x-2$

Squaring both sides we get

$x - 1 = x^2 - 4x + 4$

$\Rightarrow x^2 - 5x + 5 = 0$

Case 2 : Solve $\frac{1}{5+\sqrt{2}}$

To remove the radical, multiply the numerator and denominator by $5-\sqrt{2}$

$$= \frac{1}{5+\sqrt{2}} \times \frac{5-\sqrt{2}}{5-\sqrt{2}} = \frac{5-\sqrt{2}}{(5)^2-(\sqrt{2})^2}$$

$$= \frac{5-\sqrt{2}}{25-2} = \frac{5-\sqrt{2}}{23}$$

Q. 32 : Is 13 an inauspicious number in Mathematics too?

Ans : The superstition that 13 is associated with bad luck leads some people to fear or avoid anything involving 13. This fear is called **Triskeddekaphobia**, which leads to an interesting practice such as numbering the high rise building omitting 13. So we can say that 13 is unlucky in Mathematics but it is not the total truth. Let us discuss some features of 13 which are enough to disprove this myth.

a. There are 13 cards of Spades (♣), Hearts (♥), Diamonds (♦) and Clubs (♠) in a well shuffled pack of playing cards.

b. $13 = 7 + 6$

$= 7^2 - 6^2$

c. In a pine cone there are 13 spirals going anticlockwise and 8 in clockwise direction.

d. There is always atleast one Friday the 13th in each year. Friday the 13th is considered unlucky as it is believed that Jesus Christ was crucified on Friday the 13th.

e. There are 13 Archimedian solids.

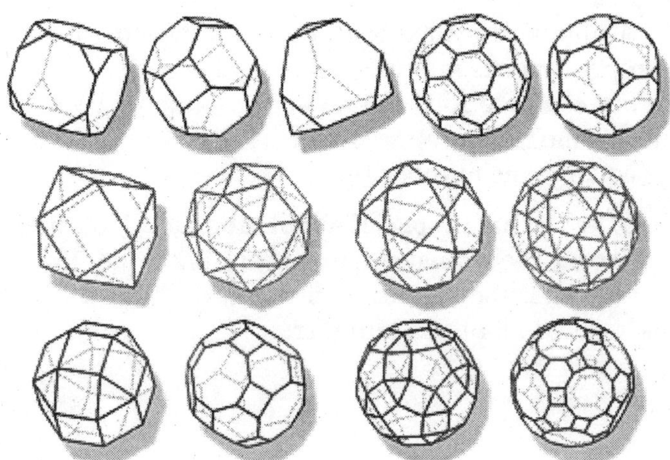

Q. 33 : What is a Perfect Number?

Ans : A number is called Perfect if it is equal to the sum of all of its factors except itself.

Example : 6, 28, 496, 8128, 33550336 and 859869056.

There are only two perfect Numbers (6, and 28) between 1 and 100. 6 has three factors 1, 2 and 3.

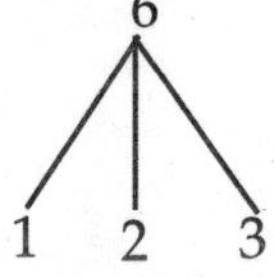

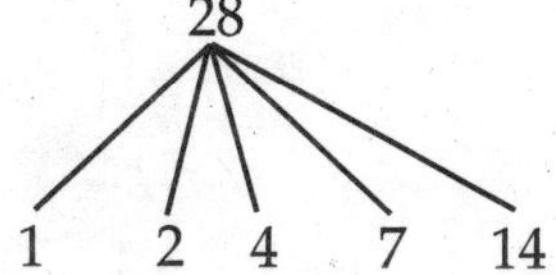

$6 = 1 + 2 + 3$

$28 = 1 + 2 + 4 + 7 + 14$

Earlier, for the philosphers such numbers had mystical and religious significance. Saint Augustine writes that although God could have created the world all at once he preferred to take 6 days as 6 is symbolised by the perfect numbers, whereas the old Testament argued that the perfection of the Universe is represented by 28, the number of days it takes the moon to complete the earth's rotation.

It is interesting to note here that it took almost 1400 years to find the fifth perfect number after the discovery of the fourth one.

A number is called Semi Perfect if the sum of some of its proper divisors is equal to the number.

For example 18 is a Semi Perfect Number because the sum of some of its proper divisors (1, 2, 3, 6, 9) *i.e.* 3 + 6 + 9 = 18 is equal to the number 18.

Q. 34 : What is special about Fibonacci Number?

Ans : The sequence of numbers 1, 1, 2, 3, 5, 8, 13......each of which after the second, is the sum of the two previous ones is called Fibonacci Number.

2 = 1 + 1
3 = 2 + 1
5 = 2 + 3
8 = 3 + 5

The Fibonacci Number is present everywhere in Nature.

1. The population of Rabbits grows in accordance to Fibonacci Series.

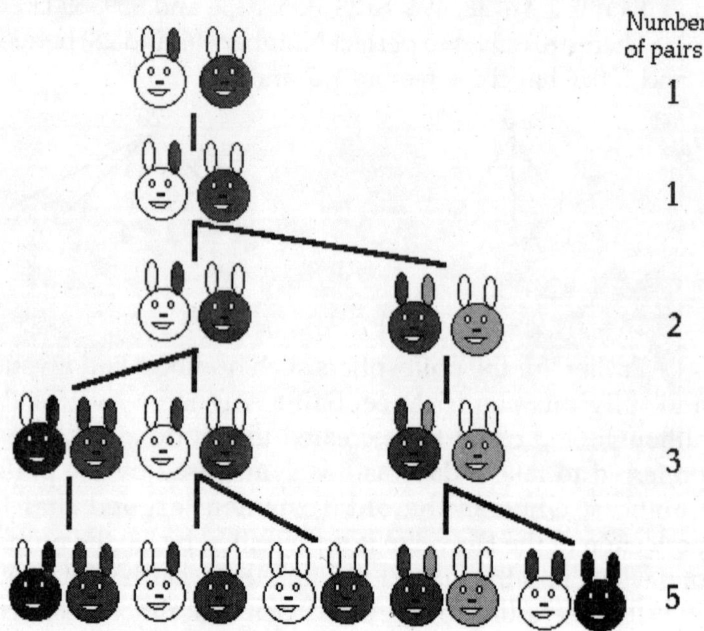

2. There are a few flowers whose petals form a Fibonacci sequence.

Name of Flowers	Number of Petals
Iris, Lily	3
Wild Rose, Columbine	5
Delphinim	8
Corn Marigold, Cineraria	13
Chicory	21

3. Pineapples and pine cones spirals in anticlockwise and clockwise direction follow Fibonacci number pattern.

Q. 35 : What is a Partition Number?

Ans : It is a number which tells us in how many ways can to a number be written as a sum of positive integers.

DEFINITION

The number of partitions p (n) of a positive integer n is the number of ways n can be written as a sum of positive integers.

$n = a_1 + a_2 + ... + a_k$

Where k is any positive integer and

$a_1 \geq a_2 \geq a_3 \geq ... \geq a_n$

Example : 5 can be written in the following ways : 5, 4 + 1, 3 + 2, 3 + 1 + 1, 2 + 2 + 1, 2 + 1 + 1 + 1 and 1 + 1 + 1 + 1 + 1 so p(5) = 7

i.e. 5 can be partitioned in 7 ways.

Indian Mathematician Ramanujan had studied partition number and given a number of methods to find the partition number.

P (n)	Number of Partitions	P(n)	Number of Partitions
P (0)	1	P (10)	42
P (1)	1	P (11)	56
P (2)	2	P (12)	77
P (3)	3	P (13)	101
P (4)	5	P (14)	135
P (5)	7	P (15)	176
P (6)	11	P (17)	231
P (7)	15	P (18)	385
P (8)	22	P (19)	490
P (9)	30	P (20)	627

Q. 36 : What is a Golden Number?

Ans : $\frac{1+\sqrt{5}}{2}$ is known as Golden number.

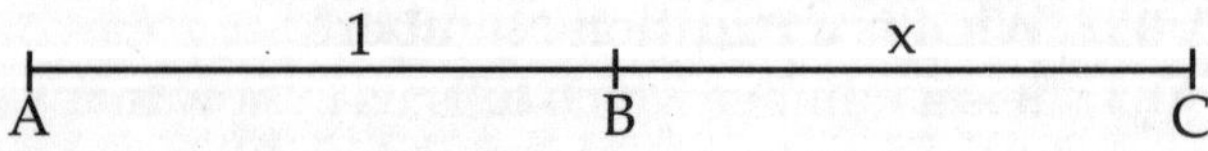

In the above line segment

Let AB = 1 and BC = x

If the ratio of the smaller part (AB) to the bigger part (BC) is equal to the ratio of the bigger part (BC) to that of the entire part (AC), then we get a constant.

The given constant is called Golden Ratio.

$$\frac{AB}{BC} = \frac{BC}{AC}$$

$$\Rightarrow \frac{1}{x} = \frac{x}{1+x}$$

$$\Rightarrow 1 + x = x^2$$

$$\Rightarrow x^2 - x - 1 = 0$$

On solving $x = \frac{(-1) \pm \sqrt{(-1)^2 - 4 \times 1 \times -1}}{2 \times 1}$

$$= \frac{1 \pm \sqrt{5}}{2}$$

Here the ratio $\frac{1+\sqrt{5}}{2}$ is called the Golden ratio or Golden number and is denoted by ϕ which is approximately equal to 1.6180339887498948482.

It occurs frequently in Geometry and Trignometry. In the shape of pentagon and decagon, phi (ϕ) occurs. It also occurs when we try to find the exact values of sines, cosines and tangents of 360^0 and 540^0. The Golden ratio can be seen in the ancient Parthenon in Athens. The Golden number has its origin from the Fibonacci numbers. Fibonacci numbers after 3 is in ratio of 1 : 16.

Q. 37 : What is a Beast Number?

Ans : 666 is called the beast number but is hardly used is mathematics. This is termed as an unpleasent number. The direct reference of number 666 can be found in the last book of Bible 'Revelation' in chapter 13, verse 18. The triple 666 is named beast because this looks like the ears of a rabbit.

In war time, this number becomes a handy tool in the hands of the propagandists. During Second World War, Hitler was ascribed with the title of beast by assigning each letter of English alphabet to a consecutive whole number beginning from 100 for A.

H = 107
I = 108
T = 119
L = 111
E = 104
R = 117
HITLER = 666

It can be written in a different combination :

666 = 1 + 2 + 3 + 4 + 567 + 89
= 123 + 456 + 78 + 9

Q. 38 : What is a Complex Number? Is complex number useful in our daily life?

Ans : Suppose we have the following equation to solve:

$x^2 + 1 = 0$

$\Rightarrow x^2 = -1$

$\Rightarrow x = \sqrt{-1}$

There is no number whose square is equal to –1. In simple words, we can say that we can't find the solution of $\sqrt{-1}$ until we define a number whose square is equal to –1. Euler defined a number i (iota) whose square is equal to –1. The **iota** is called an imaginary number. The name 'imaginary' was given by Rene Descartes in 1637.

$i^2 = -1$ $i^3 = -1$ $i^4 = 1$.......

Any number real or imaginary of the form a+ib is called complex number, where a and b are real numbers and $i^2 = -1$.

Example :

2 + 3i, –3 + 4i, 3 – 2i, –2 – 3i are examples of Complex number.

USE OF COMPLEX NUMBER

1. The electric current is produced in the coils of wire that are rotating in a magnetic field. The change in the current is represented by the number which expresses rotations. A rotation of 180^0 represents –1 and a rotation of 360^0 represents two rotations.

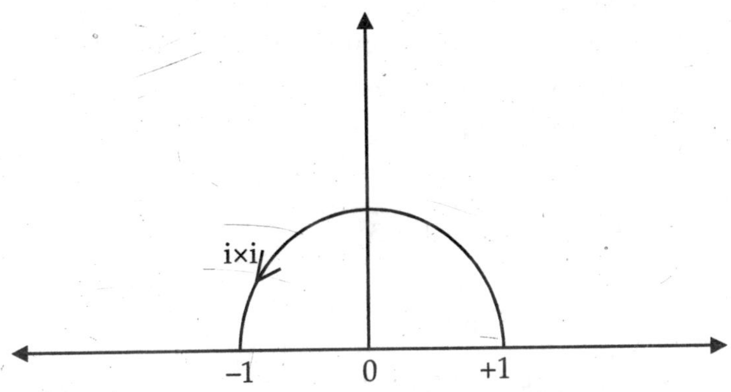

Q. 39 : How can I know, whether a decimal expansion is a terminating or non–terminating decimal?

Ans : Let us understand the concept of terminating or non–terminating decimal with examples.

$$\frac{1}{8} = 0.125$$

$$\frac{1}{4} = 0.25$$

$$= 0.3125 = \frac{5}{16}$$

The above are examples of terminating decimal expansion. Let us take 1 a few more examples.

$$\frac{1}{3} = 0.333...$$

$$\frac{2}{12} = 0.166...$$

These are the examples of non–terminating decimal expansion.

Now the question arises, how to determine whether a decimal expansion is terminating or non-terminating.

Let us generalise the examples of terminating decimals.

$$\frac{1}{8} = \frac{1 \times 125}{8 \times 125} = \frac{125}{1000} = \frac{125}{2^3 \times 5^3}$$

$$\frac{1}{4} = \frac{1}{4} \times \frac{25}{25} = \frac{25}{100} = \frac{25}{2^2 \times 5^2}$$

$$\frac{5}{16} = \frac{5 \times 625}{16 \times 625} = \frac{3125}{1000} = \frac{3125}{2^4 \times 5^4}$$

Did you notice anything?

Yes, all the decimal expansions can be kept in terminating decimal category if and only if the denominater is expressible in $2^n \times 5^m$ term, if not, they are non–terminating decimal expansions.

Q. 40 : In simplification of arithmetical calculation, VBODMAS rule is sometimes followed. Here 'O' and 'M' used for 'of' and 'Multiplication' have the same meaning *i.e.* multiplication. Why are the two letters 'O' and 'M' used instead of a single letter 'M' in VBODMAS rule?

Ans : Undoubtedly, 'O' and 'M' used for indicating 'of' and 'Multiplication' have the singular meaning but both are used in different contexts.

First let me explain what VBODMAS means :

V = Vinculum (—)

B = Brackets

( ) Parenthesis

{ } Curly Bracket

[ ] Large or Capital Bracket

O = of

D = Division

M = Multiplication

A = Addition

S = Subtraction

O used for 'of' operation indicates the fractional part of any rational number, whereas 'M' used for multiplication is taken to multiply two integers.

Example :

1. $\frac{1}{2}$ of $2 = \frac{1}{2} \times 2 = 1$

2. $\frac{3}{8}$ of $200 = \frac{3}{8} \times 200 = 75$

3. $\frac{4}{5}$ of $\frac{2}{3} = \frac{4}{5} \times \frac{2}{3} = \frac{18}{15}$

4. $12 \times 15 = 180$

5. $\frac{1}{2}$ of $8 + \{24 - 2 + (15 \div 3) - 7 \times 8\}$

$= \frac{1}{2} \times 8 + \{24 - 2 + 5 - 7 \times 8\}$

$= \frac{1}{2} \times 8 + \{24 - 2 + 5 - 56\}$

$= \frac{1}{2} \times 8 + \{29 - 58\}$

$= \frac{1}{2} \times 8 + \{-29\}$

$= 4 - 29$

$= -25$

Q. 41 : What did the primitive people use for counting?

Ans : The primitive people first used pebbles or knots or marks of ten fingers of hands for counting the number of animals in a herd.

a. Picture of Hands showing 1, 2..............9}

Suppose a person had ten sheep. Every morning when he used to let the sheep out for grazing, he would make a mark on a tree for each sheep.

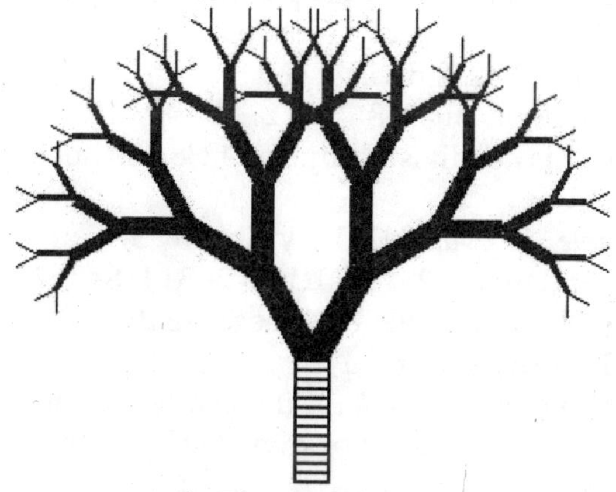

b. Picture of Tree

In the evening when he brought the sheep back, he would match each sheep with the mark on the tree to counter-check whether the sheep he had taken out for grazing had returned safely or not?

Later people developed some symbols to indicate a particular number.

Lion Head for 1
Wings of an Eagle for 2
Petal of a particular flower for 3
Four-footed animal for 4
One hand for 5, etc. etc.

Q. 42 : What are the different rules to check the divisibility of a number?

Ans : Divisibility test helps you to know whether a particular number is divisible by another small number (*e.g.* 2, 3, 4, 5, 6, 7, 8, 9, 10 and 11) or not?

Now let us learn the rule to check the divisibility of a particular number by 2 or 3 or 4 or 5 or 6, etc.

(i) Divisibility by 2 : If the last digit of a number is 0, 2, 4, 6 or 8 the whole number will be divisible by 2.

Example : 1238, 34870, 14832 are divisible by 2 as they end with 8, 0, and 2 respectively.

(ii) Divisibility by 3 : If the sum of the digits of a given number is divisible by 3 then the number itself is divisible by 3.

Example : Is 4238 divisible by 3?

Sum of digits of 4238 = 4 + 2 + 3 + 8 = 17

Since 17 is not divisible by 3 so 4238 will not be divisible by 3.

Example : Is 2348370213 divisible by 3?

Sum of digits of 2348370213 = 2+3+4+8+7+2+1+3 = 33

Since 33 is divisible by 3 because 33 = 3 + 3 = 6, so 2348370213 is divisible by 3.

(iii) Divisibility by 4 : If the last two digits (unit and tens) of any number is 00 or divisible by 4, the number is divisible by 4.

Example : Is 12342 divisible by 4?

The last two digits 42 is not divisible by 4, Hence 12342 is not divisible by 4.

Example : Is 234812 divisible by 4?

The last two digits 12 is divisible by 4, Hence 234812 is divisible by 4.

(iv) Divisibility by 5 : A number is divisible by 5 if it ends with 0 or 5.

Example : 34285, 103980...etc are divisible by 5 because 34285 has its unit digit 5 whereas 103980 ends with 0.

(v) Divisibility by 6 : A number will be divisible by 6 if it is divisible by both 2 and 3.

Example : 4248 is divisible by 6 as it is divisible by both 2 and 3.

(vi) Divisibility by 8 : A number is divisible by 8 if the last three digits is either 000 or divisible by 8.

Example : 1000 is divisible by 8 so is 2458512

1000 has 000 at the end whereas 512 of 2458512 is divisible by 8

(vii) Divisibility by 9 : A number is divisible by 9 if the sum of digits finally comes out as 9, 18, 27...

Example : 41121 is divisible by 9 as

4 + 1 + 1 + 2 +1 = 9 is divisible by 9.

(viii) Divisibility by 11 : There may be numbers of rules of divisibility of any number by 11, but I shall focus on two very common rules to check the divisibility of any number by 11.

Example : Is 51381 divisible by 11?

Rule 1 : Add the digit placed on even place and odd place separately.

b. Subtract them. If the difference is either 0 or multiple of 11, the number is divisible by 11.

5 1 3 8 1

Sum of digits at even place = 1 + 8 = 9
Sum of digits at odd place = 5 + 3 + 1 = 9
Difference = 9 – 9 = 0
So 51381 is divisible by 11.

Rule 2 : Repeatedly subtract the last digit from the remaining digit until you get the result 0.

Example : Is 51381 divisible by 11 ?
5139 – 1 = 5137
513 – 7 = 506
50 – 6 = 44
4 – 4 = 0

Hence we see that the final result comes out to be zero, so 51381 is divisible by 11.

Q. 43 : Is there any rule to check the divisibility of a number by 7?

Ans : Yes, there are many rules to check the divisibility of a number by 7.

Rule 1 :

(a) Remove the last digit and subtract twice this digit from the remaining number.

(b) Repeat this process until you get the multiple of 7.

Example : Is 18578 divisible by 7?
1857 – 2 × 8 = 1841
184 – 2 × 1 = 182
18 – 2 × 2 = 14, which is divisible by 7.
So, 18578 is divisible by 7.

Example : Is 42853 divisible by 7 ?
Solution : $4285 - 2 \times 3 = 4279$
$427 - 2 \times 9 = 409$
$40 - 2 \times 9 = 22$ is not divisible by 7
So 42853 is not divisible by 7.

Rule 2 :

(a) Add and subtract group of 3 digits starting from the right alternately. If you get the result negative, drop this sign. Repeat this process if the result is greater than 999.

(b) If not, add unit digit, 3 times the 10's digit, and 2 times the 100's digit. Repeat until you get the desired result.

Example : Is 18578 divisible by 7 ?
$578 - 018 = 560$ (Rule a)
$0 + 3 \times 6 + 2 \times 5 = 28$ (Rule b)
Since 28 is divisible by 7, so is 18578.

Example : Is 2558423 divisible by 7?
Solution : $423 - 558 + 002 = -133$ (Rule a)
Dropping the negative sign we have 133
For 133, $3 + 3 \times 3 + 2 \times 1 = 14$ (Rule b).
Since 14 is divisible by 7, so 2558423 is divisible by 7.

Rule 3 :

(a) Take the digit of the number in reverse order.

b. From right to left, multiply them successively by the digits 1, 3, 2, 6, 4, 5 ....(repeating with this sequence of 6 multipliers as long as necessary)

c. Add the digits of product obtained.

Example : Is 18578 divisible by 7?
Reverse the number 18578 you get 87581
Now follow Rule (b)
$= 8 \times 1 + 7 \times 3 + 5 \times 2 + 8 \times 6 + 1 \times 4$
$= 8 + 21 + 10 + 48 + 4$
$= 91$
Since 91 is divisible by 7 so is 18578.

Q. 44 : What is Casting Out Nines method?

Ans : Casting Out Nines is a special method to check the accuracy of addition, subtraction, multiplication, division, etc.

HOW DOES THIS METHOD WORK?

Casting Out Nines, literally means to throw nines. Now let us focus on its working.

(a) Add the digits of a number across, dropping out 9, to get a single figure. If it is not a single figure, add the digits obtained so as to get a single figure between 0 to 8.

(b) 9 is not taken into account in this process as a digit sum of 9 is the same as a digit sum of zero.

HOW TO FIND THE DIGIT SUM OF NUMBER

Example : Find the digit sum of 54653.

Verification : Digit sum of 54653 = 5 + 4 + 6 + 5 + 3 = 23

Since, 23 is a double figure number so to get a single figure we have to sum it again.

Digit sum of 23 = 2 + 3 = 5

The digit sum of 54653 can be done in other ways very easily. As discussed above, we need not take 9 into account.

Digit Sum of 54653 = $\underbrace{5 \quad +4} \quad \underbrace{+6 \quad +5 \quad +3}$

The two groups of numbers 5 + 4 and 6 + 3 can easily be left out while finding the digit sum of 54653, as their sum is equal to 9.

Example : Find the digit sum of 438219

Verification : Add all the digits

$= \underbrace{4 + 3 + \overbrace{8 + 2 + 1}} + 9 = 0$

Now, let us check the different operation.

ADDITION

Example : Verify 87643 + 38549 + 84397 + 29765 = 240354

Verification :

Digit Sum	Digit sum
87643	1
38549	2
84397	4
+29765	+2
240354	9=0

LHS : Digit of 240354 = 2 + 4 + 0 + 3 + 5 + 4 = 0

RHS : Digit sum of 1 + 2 + 4 + 2 = 0

Since LHS = RHS

Result Correct

Example : Verify 47358 + 69348 + 58769 + 38173 + 29469 = 243548

Verification :

	Digit sum
47385	0
69348	3
58769	8
38173	4
+29469	+3
243548	?

LHS : Digit sum of 243548 = 2 + 4 + 3 + 5 + 4 + 8 = 8

RHS : Sum of digit sum of numbers = 0 + 3 + 8 + 4 + 3=0

Since LHS ≠ RHS

Result Incorrect

SUBTRACTION

Example : Verify 893 – 458 = 435

Vefication :

```
  8 9 3
 –4 5 8
 ------
  4 3 5
```

Digit sum of 893 = 2

Digit sum of 458 = 8

Digit sum of 435 = 3

Since digit sum of minuend is less than the digit sum of subtrahend hence we need to replace the digit sum of 893 in such a way that the final digit sum remains the same.

Here the value of the digit sum of 893 = 2. This digit sum 2 can also be written in so many ways as the digit sum of 11, 20, 29, etc. which also gives the same value 2. Therefore the need of the hour is to replace the digit sum of 893 with any of the given values.

	Digit Sum of Number
8 9 3	11, 20, 29.......
−4 5 8	−8
4 3 5	?

LHS = Digit sum of 435 = 4 + 3 + 5 = 3
RHS = Digit sum of (11 – 8) = 3
Digit Sum of (20 – 8 = 12) = 3
Digit Sum of (29 – 8 = 21) = 3
In all the above case.
LHS = RHS
Hence result verified.

MULTIPLICATION

Multiplication is the most error-prone fundamental operation in mathematics. We know,

Multiplicand × Multiplier = Product

Example : 5972 × 4853 = 29882116

Verification :

Digit sum of multiplicand = 5 + 9 + 7 + 2 = 5
Digit sum of multiplier = 4 + 8 + 5 + 3 = 2
LHS = Digit sum of multiplicand and multiplier taken together (5 × 2 = 10) = 1
RHS : Digit sum of Product
= 2 + 9 + 8 + 8 + 2 + 1 + 1 + 6 = 1
Since LHS = RHS
Result Verified

Example : 12 × 14 = 138

Verification :

Digit Sum of multiplicand = 1 + 2 = 3
Digit Sum of multiplier = 1 + 4 = 5
LHS = Digit sum of (3 × 5 = 15) = 6
RHS = Digit sim of (138 = 1 + 3 + 8) = 3
LHS ≠ RHS
Result Incorrect

DIVISION

We know,

Dividend = Divisor × Quotient + Remainder

Let us check the division by casting out method.

Example : Verify 876543 ÷ 123, Q = 7126, R = 45

Verification : Dividend = 876543

Digit sum of Dividend = 8 + 7 + 6 + 5 + 4 + 3 = 6

Divisor = 123

Digit sum of divisor = 1 + 2 + 3 = 6

Quotient = 7126

Digit sum of Divisor 7 + 1 + 2 + 6 = 7

Remainder = 45

Digit Sum of Remainder = 4 + 5 = 0

Putting the values in given formulae we get :

LHS = Digit sum of Dividend = 6

RHS = Divisor × Quotient + Remainder

= 6 × 7 + 0

= 42

Digit sum of 42 = 6

Hence LHS = RHS

Result verified.

Q. 45 : Can animals count?

Ans : Let us begin the answer with a story reported by Sir John Lubbock, a nineteenth century astronomer and mathematician. An estate owner was bothered by a pesky crow that kept nesting in his watchtower. If the man entered the tower to dispatch the crow, the bird simply flew outside and remained there until the man left. To deceive the crow, the owner sent two men into the watch tower and had one leave. But the bird was too smart and remained outside. The next day the man repeated the operation but with three men entering and two leaving. Still the bird would not return to the tower to meet his fate. Finally, when five entered and four left, the crow was tricked and returned to the watchtower and was killed by the man sitting inside. Here the story ends with the saying that a crow can count up to four and not to five.

Otto Roehler, conducted experiments in which birds were trained to recognise various numbers of dots. Koehler concluded that birds can recognise number patterns from two to seven.

Guy Woodruff of the Primate Faculty, and David Premack, Department of Psychology, University of Pennsylvania have conducted counting research with chimpanzees. They discovered that chimpanzees can not only identify multiple objects from one to four but can also correctly identify proportions of one–fourth, one–half, three–fourths and one.

Inresearch conducted with dolphins, Louis M. Herman determined that they could remember the correct order of a string of up to eight abstract symbols.

The above description clearly indicates that animals too can sense number but they cannot be claimed to be counting scientifically.

Q. 46 : How to find rational numbers between two numbers?

Ans : Let us take the case :

Find 5 rational numbers between 2 and 3?

This can be done by changing the number as follows :

$$2 = \frac{2 \times 10}{10} = \frac{20}{10}$$

$$3 = \frac{3 \times 10}{10} = \frac{30}{10}$$

Now you need to find 5 rational numbers between $\frac{20}{10}$ and $\frac{30}{10}$ which is child's play; as they are

$$\frac{21}{10}, \frac{22}{10}, \frac{23}{10}, \frac{24}{10}, \frac{25}{10}, \frac{26}{10}, \frac{27}{10}, \frac{28}{10} \text{ and } \frac{29}{10}$$

You can find infinite many rational numbers between two consecutive natural numbers. There is also a formula, which will help you to find rational numbers between two consecutive natural numbers.

$$\text{Fomula} : p + \frac{n(q-p)}{n+1}, n = 1, 2, 3.....$$

$$\text{First number} = 2 + \frac{1(3-2)}{1+1}$$

$$= 2 + \frac{1}{2} = \frac{5}{2} \text{ [Here } p = 2, q = 3, n = 1]$$

$$\text{Second Number} = 2 + \frac{2(3-2)}{2+1}$$

$$= 2 + \frac{2}{3}$$

$$= \frac{8}{3} \text{ [} p = 2, q = 3, n = 2]$$

$$\text{Third Number} = 2 + \frac{3(3-2)}{3+1}$$

$$= 2 + \frac{3}{4} \text{ [} p = 2, q = 3, n = 3]$$

$$= \frac{11}{4}$$

$$\text{Fourth Number} = 2 + \frac{4(3-2)}{4+1}$$

$$= 2 + \frac{4}{5}$$

$$= \frac{14}{5} \text{ [} p = 2, q = 3, n = 4]$$

$$\text{Fifth Number} = 2 + \frac{5(3-2)}{5+1}$$

$$= 2+\frac{5}{6}$$

$$=\frac{7}{6}[p=2,q=3,n=5]$$

Q. 47 : Can numbers be categorised on the basis of the name of mathematicians?

Ans : Yes, there are many numbers in mathematics which bear the name of mathematicians.

They are :

a. Ramanujan Number : 1729

$1729 = 10^3 + 9^3$

$= 12^3 + 1^3$

b. Euler Number : 635318657

$635318657 = 133^4 + 134^4$

$= 59^4 + 158^4$

c. Kaprekar Number : 6174. Dr. D.R. Kaprekar, a famous Indian Mathematician discovered it.

Take any four-digit number where all digits are not equal. Arrange these numbers in descending order and then reverse it. Subtract the two. Repeat the process until you get the same number coming after each operation. Certainly you will get 6174.

d. Fermat Number : After the name of Pierre de Fermat, a French amateur mathematician

$F_n = 2^{2^n} + 1$ for n = 1, 2, 3.......

e. Fibonacci Number : Fibonacci was renowned mathematician of Italy. In the Fibonacci number, every next number is the sum of the previous two.

1, 1, 2, 3, 5, 8, 13,21, 34, 55...............are the Fibonacci numbers.

f. Liouville Number : Any number of the form

$$\sum_{n=1}^{\infty}\frac{A}{10^{n!}}$$

Where A is any constant is called Liouville number. Liouville was a French analyst and Geometer.

g. Pythagorean Number : Any set of positive integers satisfying the equation

$x^2 + y^2 = z^2$ **is called Pythagorean triplet.**

The set of Pythagorean numbers are—

(3, 4, 5) (5, 12, 13) (6, 8 ,10) (7, 24, 25) (8, 15, 17) (9, 40, 41) (11, 60, 61).........

h. Lucas Number : 2, 1, 3, 4, 7, 11, 18, 29, 47, 76, 123, 199, 322, 521.........are Lucas Number.

$L_n = L_{n-1} + L_{n-2}$

For $n > 1$

Edward Lucas was a French mathematician. Lucas numbers also follows the rule of Fibonacci. Here the next number after 1 is the sum of preceeding two.

$4 = 1 + 3$, $7 = 3 + 4$..................etc.

i. Mersenne Number :

$M_n = 2^p - 1$ is called Mersenne Number, where p = 2, 3, 5, 7, 13, 17, 19, 31 and 67. Marin Mersenne was a monk in a church.

There might be many of such numbers which bear the name of mathematicians but discussing all does not seem viable.

Q. 48 : What is the rule to find primes between two numbers?

Ans : There is no proper method to find primes between two numbers, except the sieve of Eratosthenes. Eratosthemes of Alexandria (276–194 BC) was a Greek astronomer, geographer, philosopher and mathematician.

SIEVE OF ERATOSTHENES

The process of determining all the primes not greater than a number N by writing down all the numbers from 2 to N, removing those after 2 which are the multiples of 2, those after 3, which are the multiples of 3, multiples of primes themselves have been removed, only prime number will remain.

Suppose you have to find the primes between 1 to 20.

(a) Write down all numbers from 1 to 20.

(b) Take the square root of 20 *i.e.* $\sqrt{20}$ = 4.5 (approx). Hence you need to remove all multiples of primes not greater than 5.

②	③	~~4~~	⑤
~~6~~	~~7~~	~~8~~	~~9~~
~~10~~	11	~~12~~	13
~~14~~	~~15~~	~~16~~	17
~~18~~	19	~~20~~	

(c) Circle 2, 3, and 5 and strike all the multiples of 2, 3, 5.

d. Whatever left including 2, 3, 5 are primes.

Hence primes between 2 to 20 are

2, 3, 5, 7, 11, 13, 17 and 19.

❑

GEOMETRY

Q. 1 : What is Geometry. What are its different types?

Ans : Geometry is a science that treats the shape and size of things. There are different types of geometry. They are :

i) Euclidean Geometry
ii) Analytical Geometry
iii) Non–Euclidean Geometry
iv) Plane–Analytical Geometry
v) Solid Geometry
vi) Projective Geometry
vii) Plane (Elementary) Geometry

Euclid is the father of Geometry and the rest followed later.

Q. 2 : What do you mean by a polygon?

Ans : A plane figure consisting of n points where $n \geq 3$ is called polygon.

Sides	Name
3	Triangle
4	Quadrilateral
5	Pentagon
6	Hexagon
7	Heptagon
8	Octagon
9	Nonagon
10	Decagon
12	Dodecagon

Q. 3 : What is the difference between convex and concave polygon?

Ans : **Convex Polygon :** A polygon is convex, if it lies on one side of any line that contains a side of the polygon *i.e.* if each interior angle is less than or equal to 180^0.

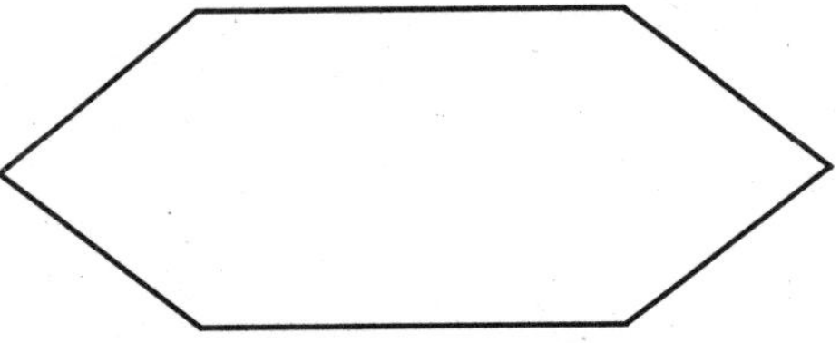

CONCAVE POLYGON

A polygon is concave if it is not convex. *i.e.* if at least one of its interior angles is greater than 180°.

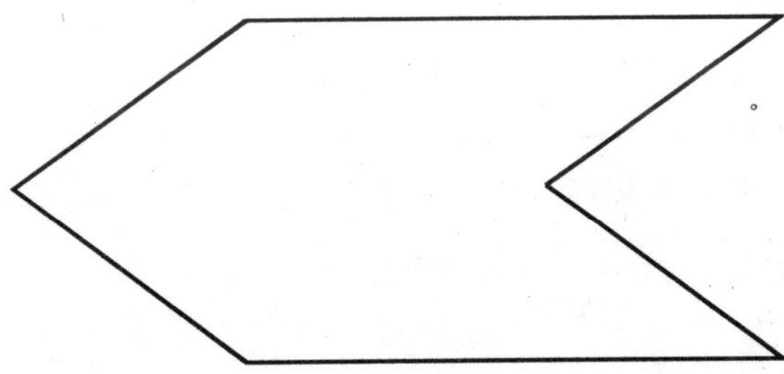

Q. 4 : Define angles. What are its different types?

Ans : **Angle :** The inclination subtended by joining two rays with a single vertex is known as angle.

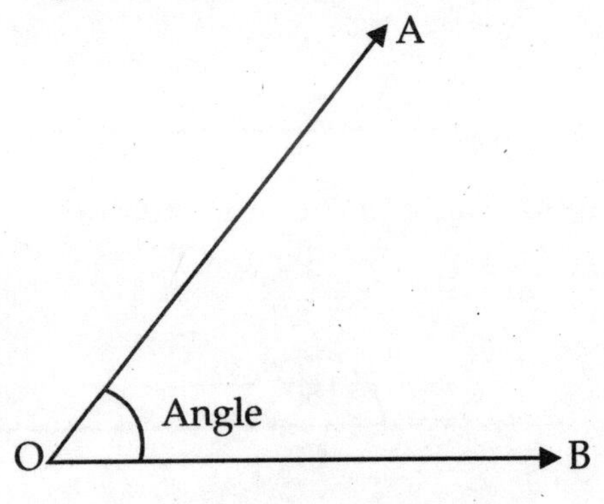

Here OA and OB are the two rays with common vertex, forming $\angle AOB$

TYPES OF ANGLES

i) Acute Angle : If the measure of angle is less than 90°.

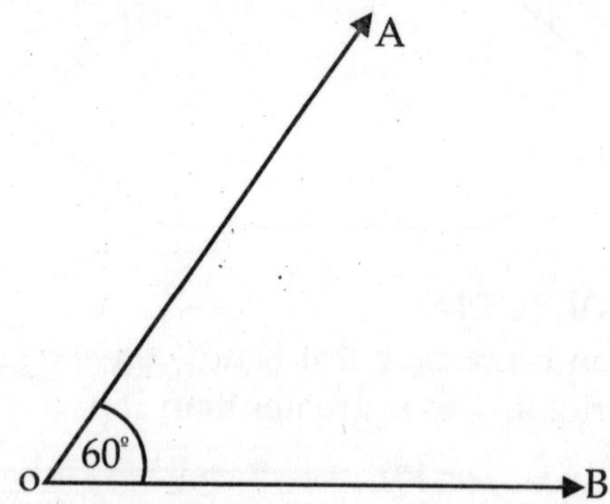

ii) Obtuse angle : When the measure of an angle is more than 90° but less than 180°.

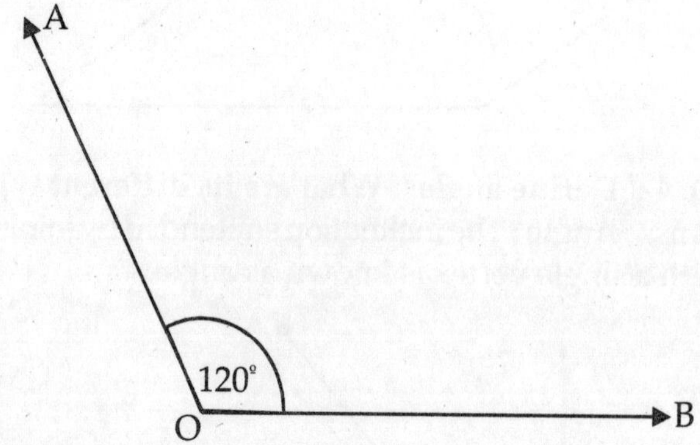

iii) Straight Angle : When the measure of an angle is 180°.

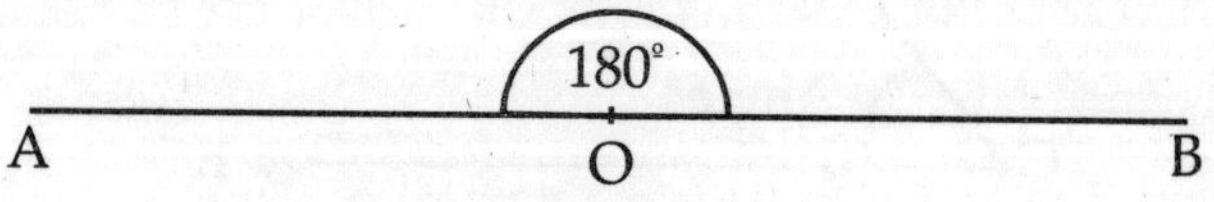

iv) Right Angle : When the measure of an angle is equal to 90°.

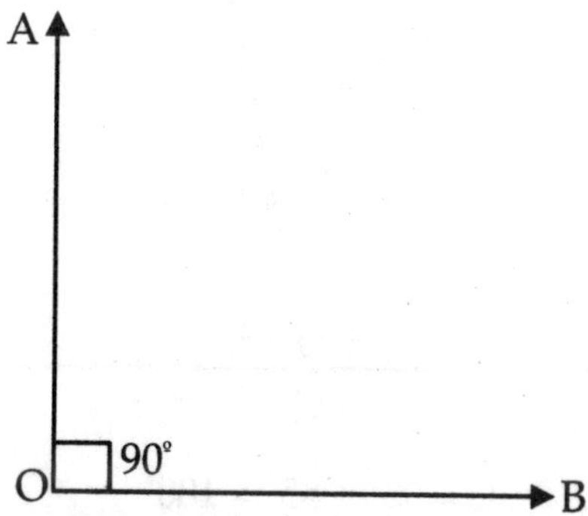

v) Reflex Angle : When the measure of an angle is more than 180° but less than 360°.

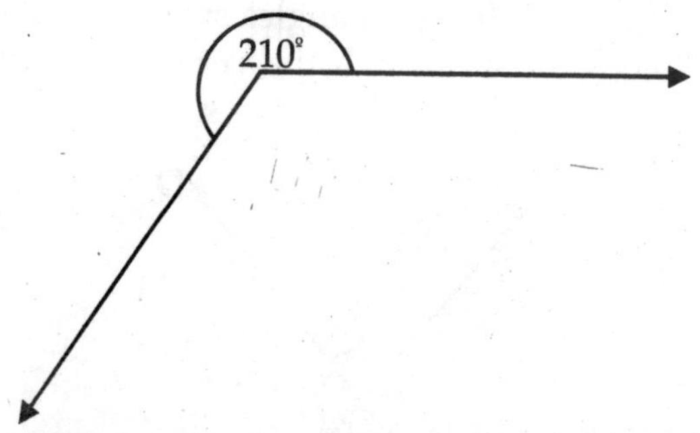

vi) Complementary Angle : When the sum of two angles is equal to 90°.

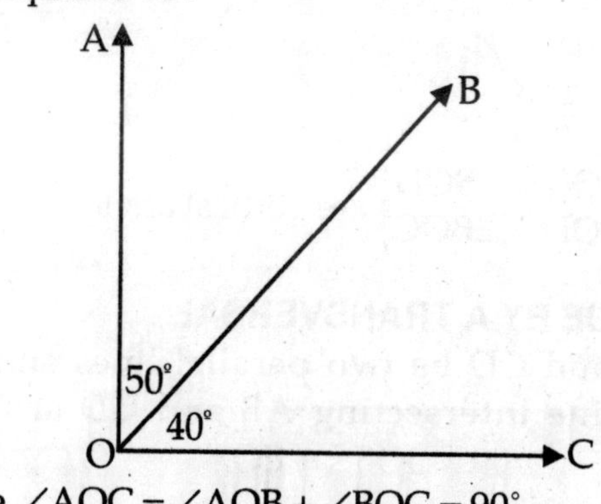

Here $\angle AOC = \angle AOB + \angle BOC = 90^\circ$

vii) Supplementary Angle : When the sum of two angles is equal to 180°.

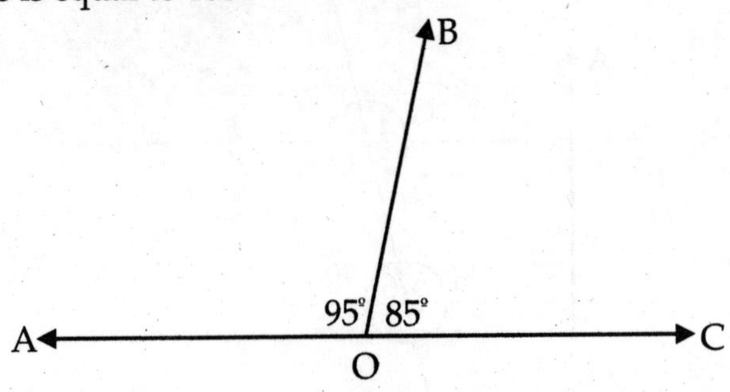

$\angle AOB + \angle BOC = 95^\circ + 85^\circ = 180^\circ$

viii) Conjugate Angles : Two angles whose sum is equal to 360° are called Conjugate angles.

ix) Vertical Angle : Two angles such that each side of one is a prolongation, through the vertex, of a side of the other.

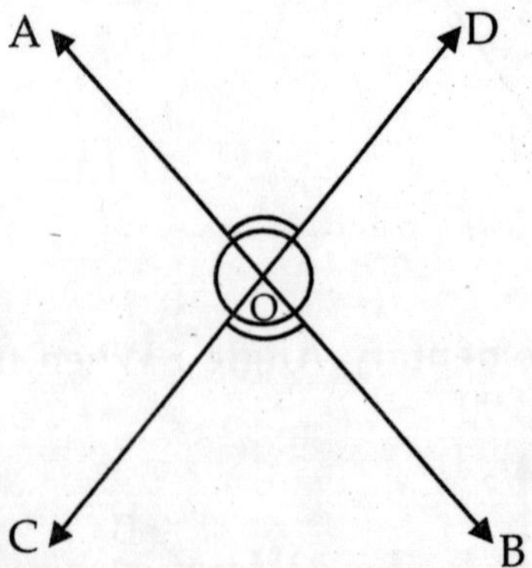

Here $\left.\begin{matrix}\angle AOC = \angle BOD \\ \angle AOD = \angle BOC\end{matrix}\right\}$ are vertical angles.

ANGLES MADE BY A TRANSVERSAL

Let AB and CD be two parallel lines and EF is a transversal line intersecting AB and CD at G and H respectively.

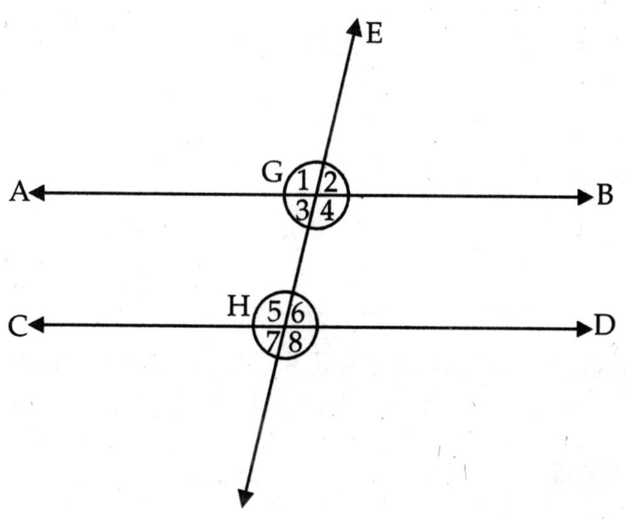

$$\left.\begin{array}{l}\angle 1=\angle 4\\ \angle 2=\angle 3\\ \angle 5=\angle 8\\ \angle 6=\angle 7\end{array}\right\}\text{Verticaly opposite angles}$$

$$\left.\begin{array}{l}\angle 2=\angle 6\\ \angle 1=\angle 5\\ \angle 3=\angle 7\\ \angle 4=\angle 8\end{array}\right\}\text{Corresponding angles}$$

$$\left.\begin{array}{l}\angle 4=\angle 5\\ \angle 3=\angle 6\end{array}\right\}\text{Alternate angles}$$

Q. 5 : What is the difference between centroid, incentre, orthocentre and circumcentre?

Ans : **Centroid** : The point of intersection of all the medians is called-centroid.

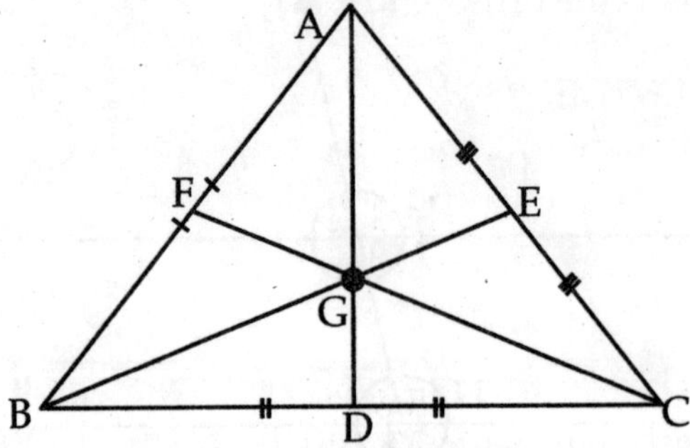

Here G is the centroid because it is the point of intersection of all three medians AD, BE and CF.

INCENTRE

The point of intersection of all the angle bisectors is called the Incentre.

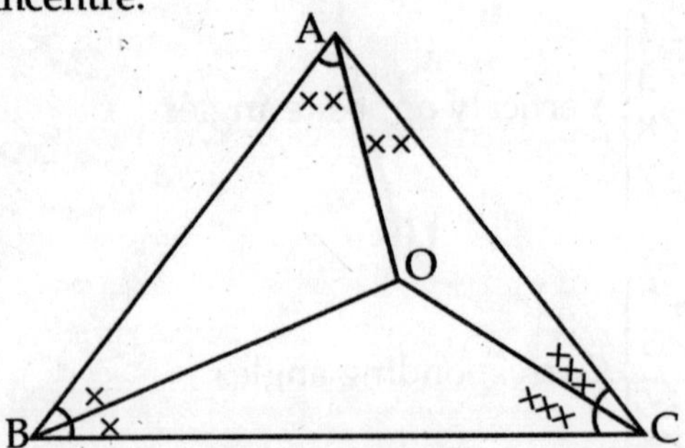

AO, BO and CO are bisectors of $\angle A$, $\angle B$ and $\angle C$ which meet at O. Here O is the Incentre.

Orthocentre : The point of intersection of the three altitudes of the triangle is called Orthocentre.

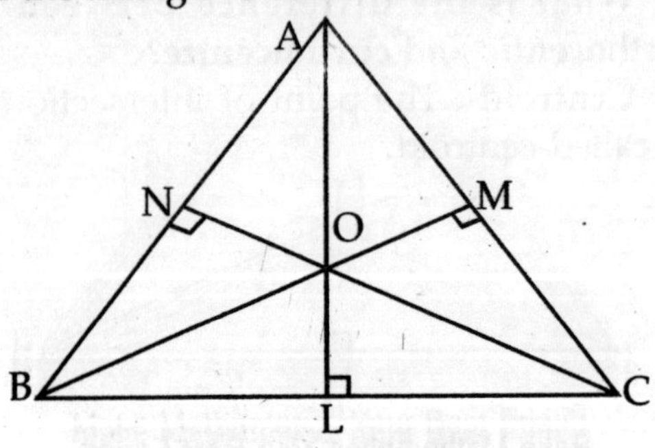

Here O is the orthocentre.

CIRCUMCENTRE

The centre of the circumscribed circle is the Circumcentre. It is the point of intersection of the perpendicular bisectors of the sides.

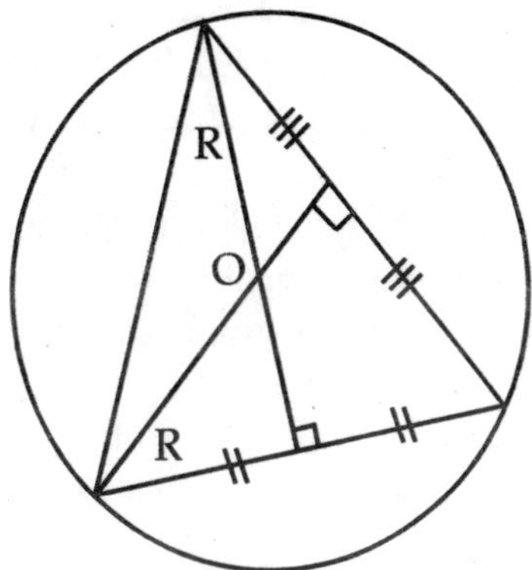

Q. 6 : Is the sum of angles of a triangle always equal to 180° ?

Ans : In Euclidean Geometry, the sum of the angles of a triangle always comes to 180°. You can prove it by some activities.

Draw three triangles of different shape and size namely:

(i) Acute Angle Triangle

(ii) Obtuse Angle Triangle

(iii) Right Angle Triangle

Measure all the angles and sum them up. Did you come to the point that sum of angles of triangle is equal to 180°?

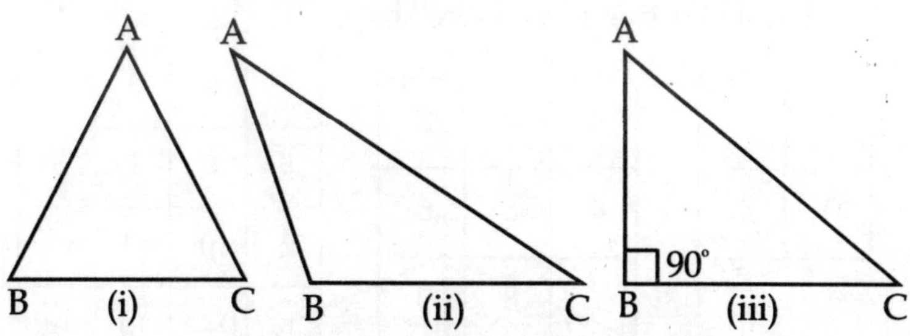

Figure	∠A	∠B	∠C	∠A + ∠B + C	Conclusion
1	60°	60°	60°	180°	sum of the
2	45°	90°	45°	180°	angles of a
3	30°	110°	40°	180°	triangle =180°

But the fifth postulate of Euclid had given the way to find a new branch of Geometry popularly known as Non–Euclidean Geometry.

In Lobachevsky–Bolyai Geometry, the sum of angles of the triangle is always less than 180°, whereas in Riemannian Geometry, the sum of angles of a triangle is always grater than 180^0.

Lobachevsky–Bolyai Geometry is based on the assumption that at least two lines can be drawn through a given point parallel to a given point; on the other hand the Riemannian Geometry is based on the assumption that no lines are ever parrallel drawn through a fixed point manually at right angles to each other.

Q. 7 : Are there any numbers which exhibit the geometrical shape in Mathematics?

Ans : Yes, there are several figurative numbers which are in the shape of geometrical figures such as Triangle, Square, Rectangle, Tetrahedral, Pentagon, Hexagon etc. Let us discuss the figurative numbers one by one.

(a) Square Numbers : 1, 4, 9, 16, 25............are called the square numbers. It is the number of dots arranged in such a way that it represents a square shape.

1	2
3	4

1	2	3
4	5	6
7	8	9

1	2	3	4
5	6	7	8
9	10	11	12
13	14	15	16

(b) Triangular Numbers : 1, 3, 6, 10, 15..........are triangular numbers because they from the shape of a triangle.

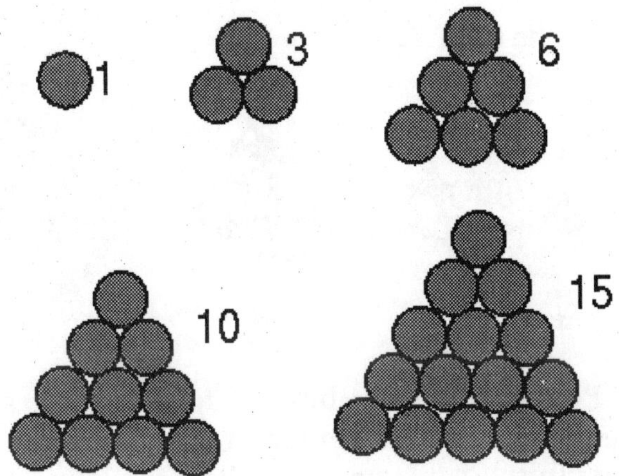

(c) Cubic Numbers : The numbers which can be represented by three-dimensional cubes are called cubic numbers. 1, 8, 27, 64, 125.......are cubic numbers which are obviously the cubes of 1, 2, 3, 4, 5..............

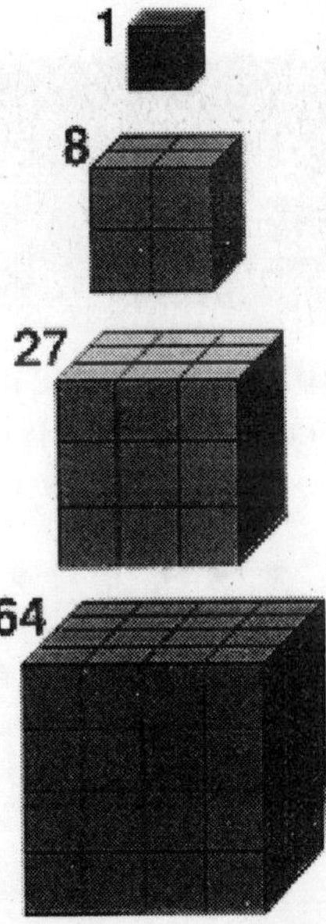

(d) Tetrahedral Numbers : The numbers that can be represented by layers of triangles forming a tetrahedron shape are called tetrahedral numbers. It is a figurative number of the form $T_{-} = n_{-}$

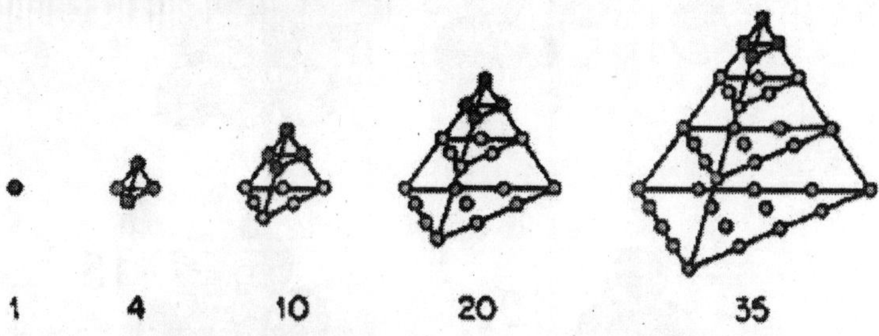

e. Pentagonal Numbers : Those numbers which represent the shape of pentagon are called pentagonal numbers. In the pentagonal numbers the lower base is a square with a triangle on the top.

1, 5, 12, 22, 35..........are an example. The nth pentagonal number P_n is given by the formula

$$P_n = \frac{n(3n-1)}{2}$$

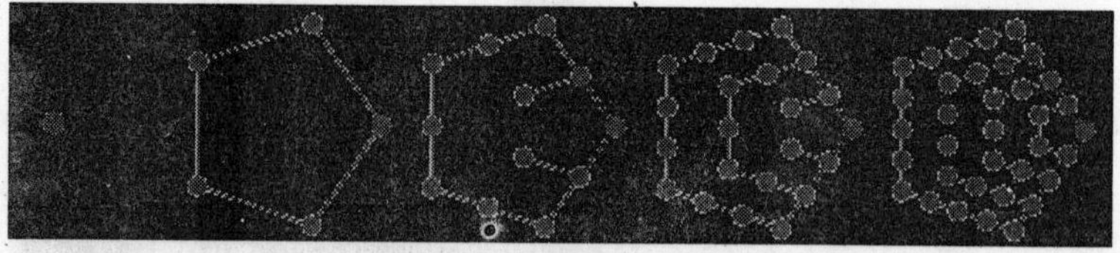

f. Hexagonal Numbers : Those numbers which form a shape of hexagon are called hexagonal numbers. 1,6, 15, 28, 45.........

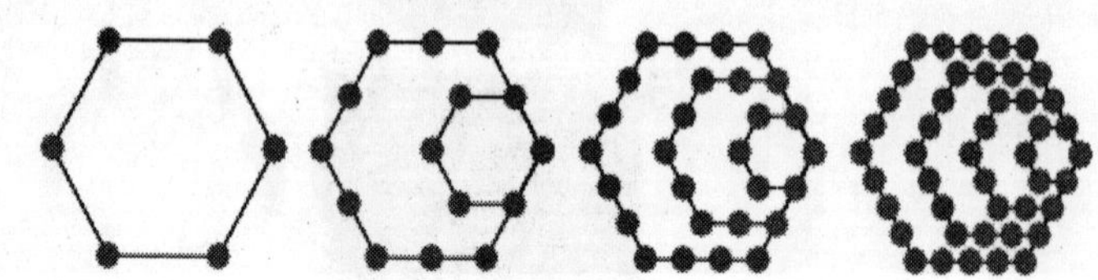

(g) Pyramidal Numbers : Those numbers which can be represented as layers of squares forming a pyramid as called pyramidal numbers. Example : 35, 55

Q. 8 : What is a quadrilateral? Discuss its different types.

Ans : A polygon having four sides is called a quadrilateral.

TYPES OF QUADRILATERAL

(a) Square
(b) Rectangle
(c) Rhombus
(d) Parallelogram
(e) Trapezoid

Square : A quadrilateral with equal sides and equal angles.

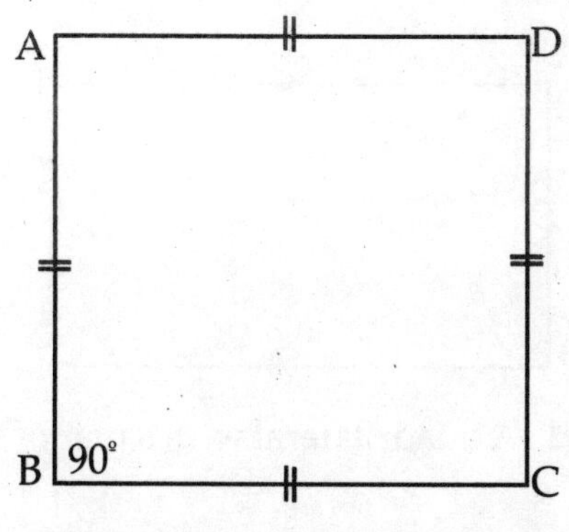

Rectangle : A quadrilateral with opposite sides equal and all angles equal to 90°.

Rhombus : A quadrilateral with all sides equal but none of the angles equal to 90°.

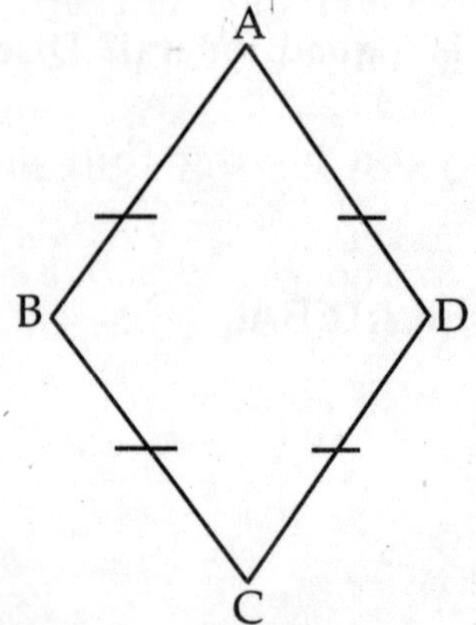

Parallelogram : A quadrilateral with opposite sides equal and parallel

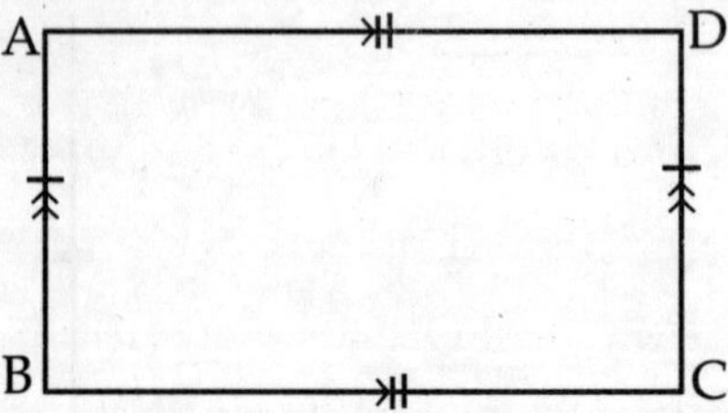

Trapezoid : A quadrilateral with a pair of sides parallel.

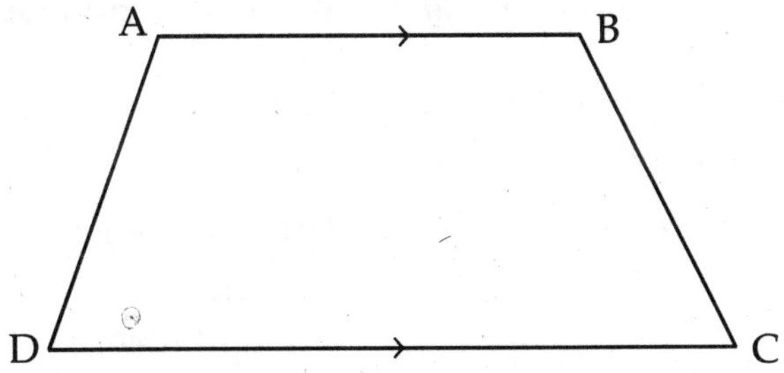

Q. 9 : What does QED and CPCT stand for?

Ans : The word QED commonly found at the end of proof of theorem in Geometry stands for *quod erat demonstrandum* (that which was to be proven). Euclid used to conclude his proof with the word *haper edei deiksai* which when translated in Latin by the medieval geometers changed to *quod erat demonstrandum* (QED). The first known use of QED in print appears in 1505 in the translation of Euclid by Bartholemew Zamberti.

CPCT stands for congruence part of congruent triangle. This means that when two triangles are congruent, all its parts will be equal to one another.

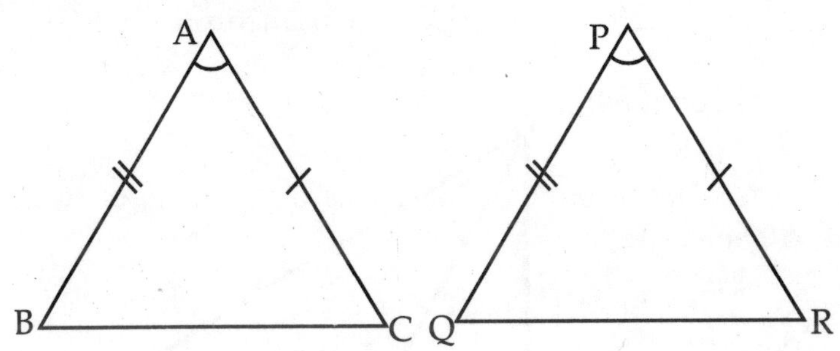

In ΔABC and ΔPQR

if $AB = PQ$, $\angle A = \angle P$ and $AC = PR$

Hence, $\Delta ABC \cong \Delta PQR$

Therefore by CPCT $\quad BC = QR$

$\angle B = \angle Q$

and $\angle C = \angle R$

Q. 10 : What is the difference between Polygon and Polyhedron?

Ans : A plane figure consisting of n points where $n \geq 3$ is called Polygon.

Sides	Name of Polygon
3	Triangle
4	Quadrilateral
5	Pentagon
6	Hexagon

Whereas a solid bounded by plane polygons is polyhedron. The bonding polygons are the faces and the intersection of the faces are the edges, the point where three or more edges intersect are the vertices.

Faces	Name of Polyhedron
4	Tetrahedron
6	Hexahedron
8	Octahedron
12	Dodecahedron
20	Icosahedron

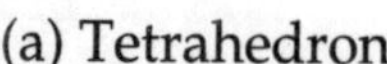
(a) Tetrahedron

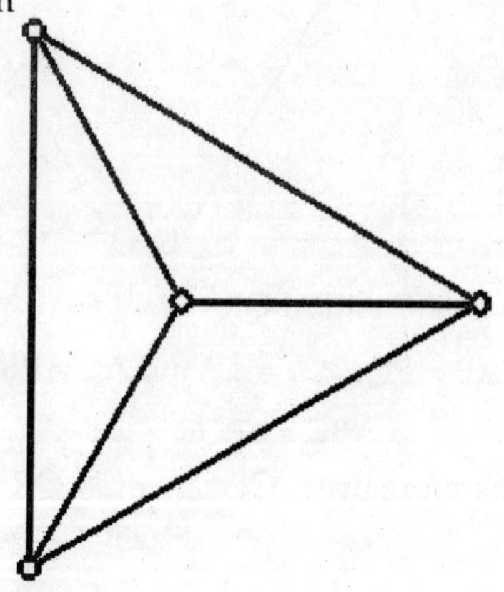

(b) Dodecahedron

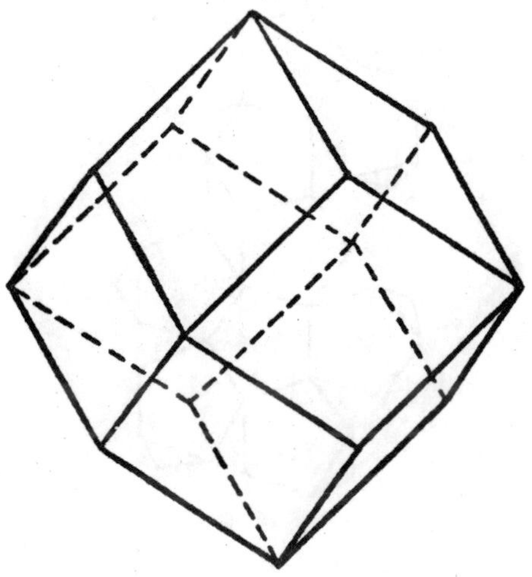

(c) Icosahedron

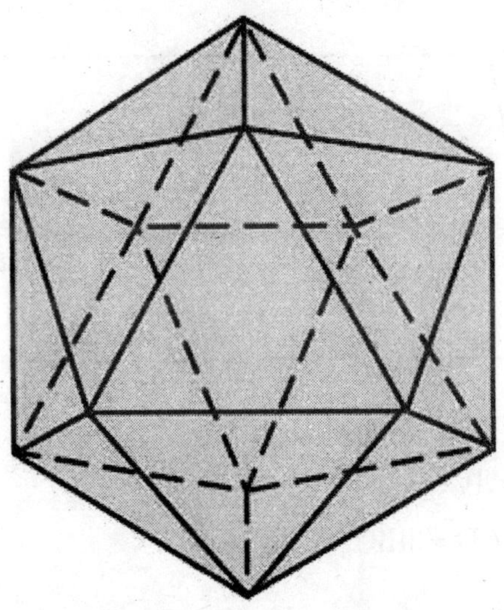

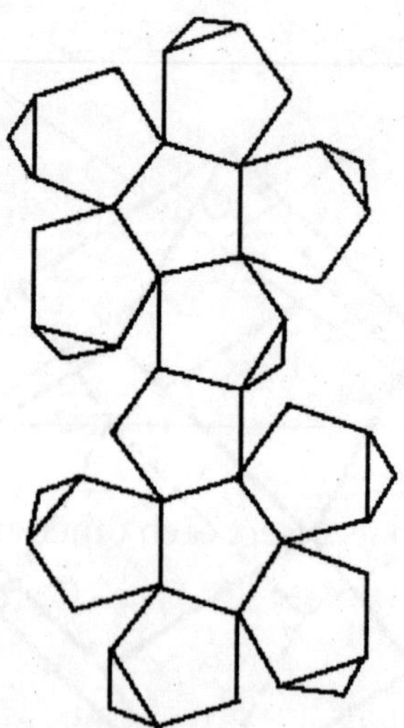

Q. 11 : What is the difference between parallelogram and parallelepiped.

Ans : **Parallelogram :** A quadrilateral with its opposite sides equal and parallel is known as parallelogram.

PROPERTIES OF PARALLELOGRAM

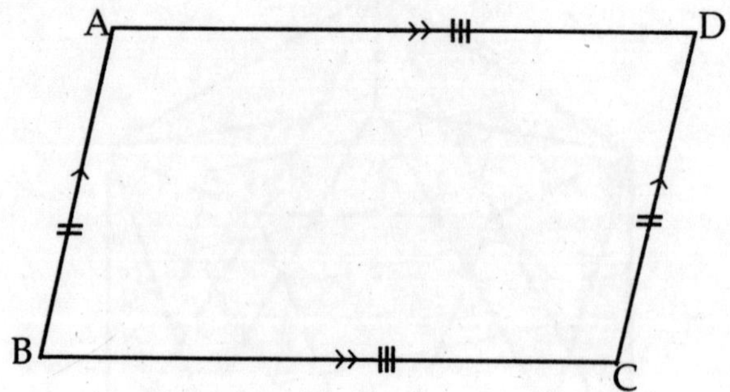

(i) ABCD is parallelogram if

AB = || CD

and AD = ||| BC

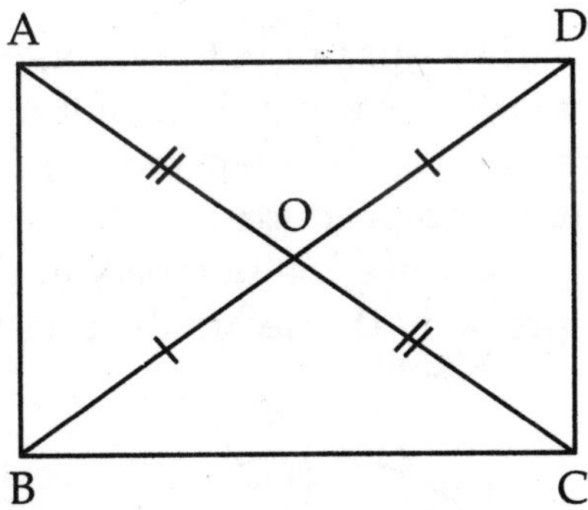

(ii) The diagonals bisect each other at O

$AO = OC$
$BO = OD$

(iii) The diagonals are not of equal length

$AC \neq BD$

(iv) Opposite angles are equal

$\angle A = \angle C$ and $\angle B = \angle D$

Parallelepiped : A prism whose bases are parallelograms; a polyhedron, all of whose faces are parallelograms. The faces other than the bases are **lateral faces**. The diagonal of a parallelepiped is a line segment joining two vertices which are not in the same face.

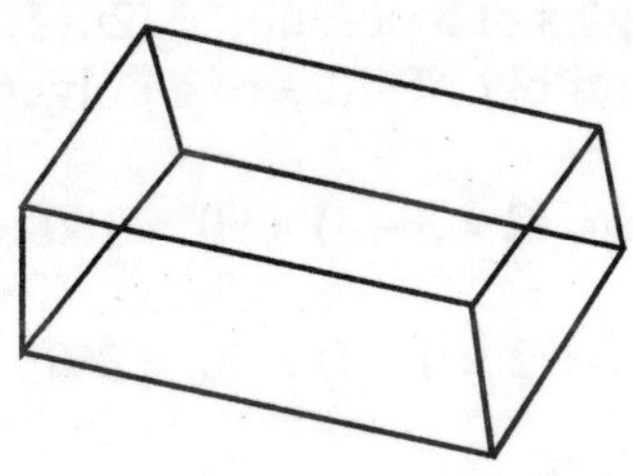

Q. 12 : Why is the angle of a circle 360°?

Ans : According to Otto Neugebauer—a second Egyptian contribution to Astronomy is the division of the day into 24 hours, though these hours were originally not of even length but were dependent upon the seasons. A little further he says, "Thus our present division of the day into 24 hours of 60 minutes each is the result of a Hellenistic (Greek) modification of an Egyptian practice combined with Babylonian numerical procedures.

Babylonians used base 60 numbers in their business, astronomy and probably this led to the division of a circle into 360 parts.

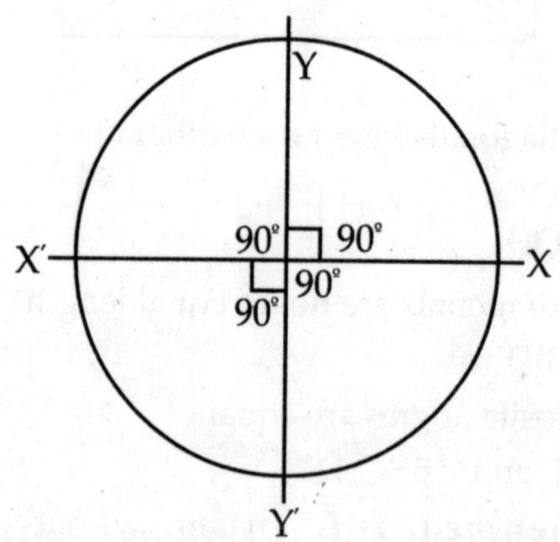

Q. 13 : How can you decide the angle sum of a Polygon?

Ans : The angle sum of any polygon can be found by means of the given formula.

Sum of all angles of a polygon = (2n–4) × Rt. Angle
(Where n = number of sides of a polygon.)
Let n = 3
Sum of angles = $(2 \times 3 - 4) \times 90^\circ = 180^\circ$
Let n = 4
Sum of angles = $(2 \times 4 - 4) \times 90^\circ = 360^\circ$
Let n = 5
Sum of angles = $(2 \times 5 - 4) \times 90^\circ = 540^\circ$
Let n = 6
Sum of angles = $(2 \times 6 - 4) \times 90^\circ = 720^\circ$
Let n = 8
Sum of angles = $(2 \times 8 - 4) \times 90^\circ = 1080^\circ$

In order to find the exterior angle of any polygon you can apply the given formula.

$$\text{Exterior Angle} = \frac{360}{n}$$

$$\text{Exterior angle of a Pentagon} = \frac{360}{5} = 72^\circ$$

$$\text{Interior angle of a Regular polygon} = \frac{(2n-4)\times 90}{n}$$

For n = 5

$$\text{Each interior angle} = \frac{2\times 5-4)\times 90}{5}$$

$$= \frac{6\times 90}{5}$$

$$= 6\times 18 = 108^\circ$$

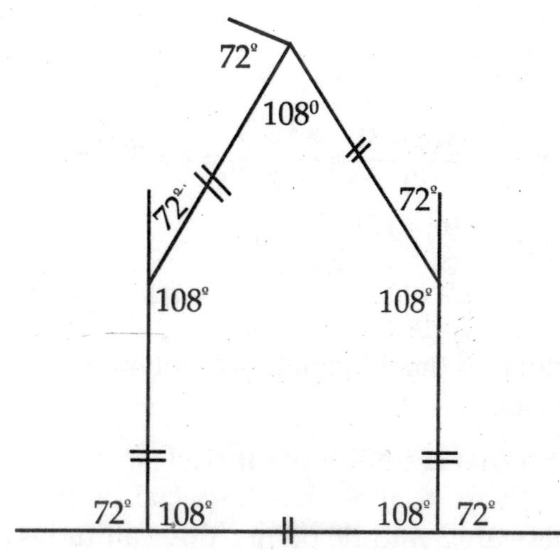

So, you can conclude from the above explanation that sum of exterior angles of any polygon = 360°

Q. 14 : What is the formula to find the number of diagonals of a Polygon?

Ans : The number of diagonals of a polygon with n sides = $\frac{n(n-3)}{2}$.

The diagonal is a straight line joining the two end points of a polygon. So, out of n sides of a polygon, the number of diagonals = $n_{c_2} - n$

$$= \frac{n(n-1)}{2} - n$$

$$= \frac{n^2 - 3n}{2} = \frac{n(n-3)}{2}$$

Let us find the diagonals in different types of polygon:

Quadrilateral (n = 4)

$$\text{Diagonal} = \frac{4(4-3)}{2} = 2$$

Hexagon (n = 6)

$$\text{Diagonal} = \frac{6(6-3)}{2} = \frac{6 \times 3}{32} = 9$$

Octagon (n = 8)

$$\text{Diagonal} = \frac{8(8-3)}{2} = \frac{8^4 \times 5}{2} = 4 \times 5 = 20$$

Dodecagon (n = 12)

$$\text{Diagonal} = \frac{12(12-3)}{2} = \frac{12 \times 9}{2} = 6 \times 9 = 54$$

You can find the diagonals of a polynomial having any number of sides.

Q. 15 : What are Nine-point circles?

Ans : Every triangle has 9 special points associated with it. These are 3 middle points, three altitudes and three middle points of lines joining vertices to the orthocentre of the triangle, and all these nine points lie on a circle called Nine–point circles.

In the above picture D, E, F are the mid–points of the sides AB, BC and AC. CL, AM and BN are the altitudes drawn from the vertex C, A and B on the opposite sides. O is the orthocentre. Moreover, X, Y and Z are the mid–points of AO,

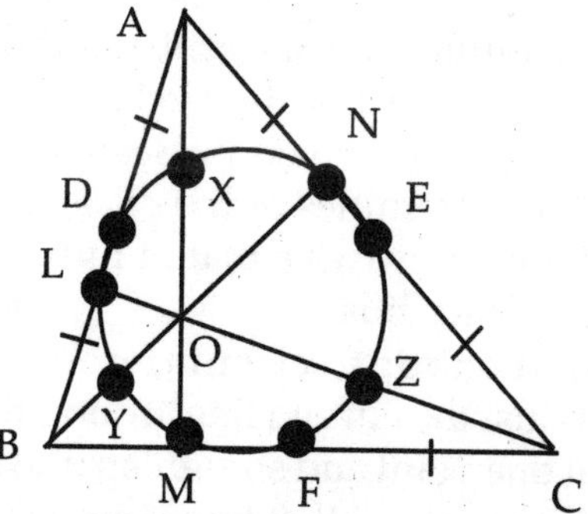

BO and CO. The nine–points D, E, F, L, M, N, X, Y, Z lie on a circle. This result was known to Euler in 1765 but re–discovered by Feverbach in 1822. The resulting circle is known as Feverbach circle or Nine–point circle.

Q. 16 : Why do we have 60 seconds in a minute?

Ans : The Babylonean civilisation had their number system with a base 60. It seems that they had chosen the base 60 as it could be factored into many numbers. Moreover, the word second comes from the second sexagesimal place in the base 60 expansion.

Q. 17 : Is circle a polygon?

Ans : No, circle is not a polygon. A polygon is composed of a finite set of straight line segments, and a circle is obviously not. But one can make a polygon which is as close to a circle. But construction of such polygon is only an imagination.

Q. 18 : What is a circumference? How can the circumference of a circle be worked out?

Ans : The circumference of a circle is the distance around it.

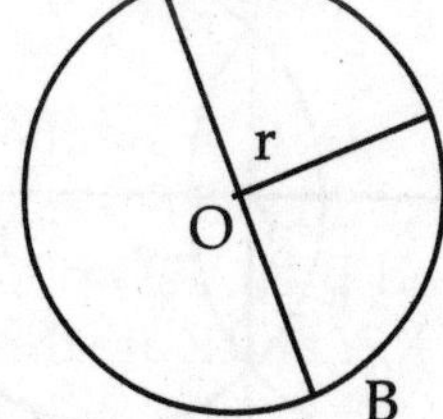

In the above figure, O is the centre and r is the distance between centre to one end of the circle. It is called Radius. There is one special line which passes through the centre and joins both the extremities of the circle, called diameter. The length of diameter is twice that of radius.

Diameter = 2 × Radius

Now, what about circumference? Well, the circumference is just the curved line around the circle. If you cut your circle at one point and straighten it so that it becomes a straight line, the length of that line is going to be the length of the circumference.

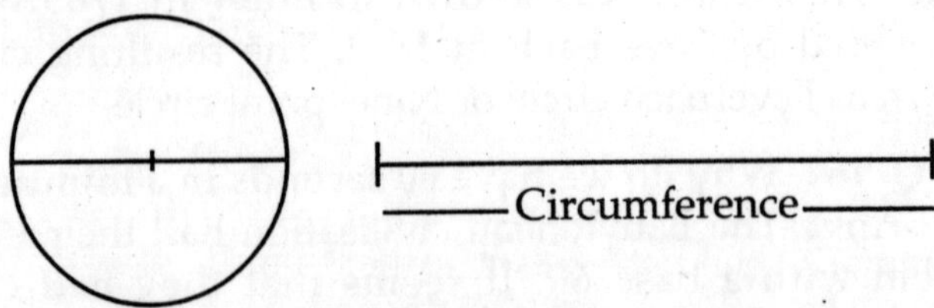

Now if you take the diameter of any circle, the circumference of it is around 3 times, but not exactly.

Mathematically, it is $\frac{22}{7} \times$ Diameter

Circumference = $2\pi r$

$= \pi d$

Q. 19 : Let AB be a line segment. Why do we take the arc length half or more than half while bisecting the line segment into two equal halves?

Ans : Take a line AB. Taking A and B as centre draw two circles, so that they intersect at two points.

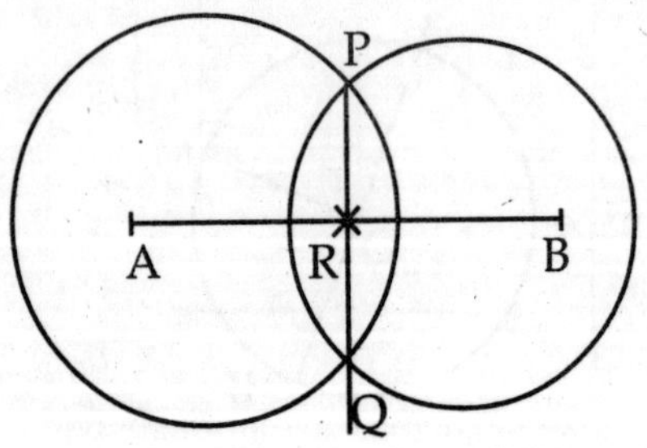

If the arc length taken from A and B is less than half the length of line–segment, they will not intersect at two points. Hence the perpendicular bisector of a line–segment cannot be drawn.

The basic principle of taking the arc length half or more than half lies in the fact that two circles can only intersect if the arc length is half or more than half.

Q. 20 : What is the origin of Degree?

Ans : In 1936, a tablet was excavated some 200 miles from Babylon. This tablet was partially translated in 1950, and is devoted to various geometrical figures and states that the ratio of perimeter of a regular hexagon to the circumference of the circumscribed circle equals number which in modern notation is given by $\frac{57}{60}+\frac{36}{60^2}$.

This shows that Babylonians used the sexagesimal system, *i.e.* their base was 60 rather than 10. The Babylonians knew, of course, that the perimeter of a hexagon is exactly equal to six times the radius of circumscribed circle. In fact, that was evidently the reason why they chose to divide the circle into 360°.

The division of a circle into 360 parts is equal to 1 degree.

Q. 21 : For the point P (x_1, y_1) and Q (x_2, y_2) why is the distance between PQ = $\sqrt{(x_2-x_1)^2+(y_2-y_1)^2}$

Ans :

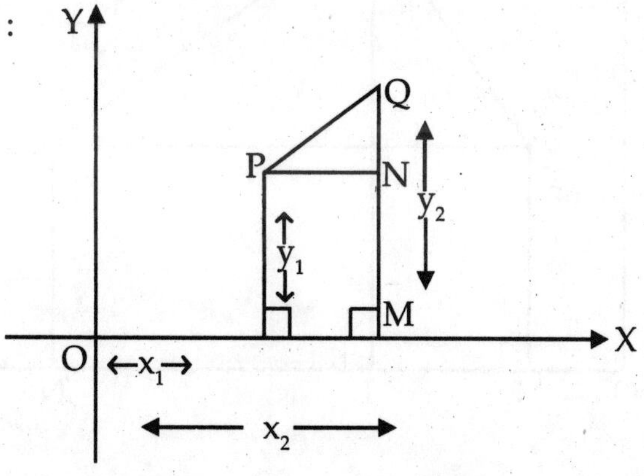

Y

Q

P

N

y_2

y_1

M

X

O $\leftarrow x_1 \rightarrow$

$\longleftarrow x_2 \longrightarrow$

Let P $(x_1 y_1)$ and Q (x_2, y_2) be two points in a plane. Draw PL and QM perpendicular on x–axis

$OL = x_1 \quad OM = x_2$

$PL = y_1 \quad QM = y_2$

Drop PN $\perp$ QM.

$\Rightarrow ML = x_2 - x_1 = PN$

and $QN = y_2 - y_1$

Now, In Δ PQN

$PQ^2 = PN^2 + QN^2$

$= (x_2 - x_1)^2 + (y_2 - y_1)^2$

$\Rightarrow PQ = \sqrt{(x_2 - x_1)^2 + (y_2 - y_1)^2}$

Q. 22 : For the triangle ABC, with vertex A $(x_1 y_1)$, B (x_2, y_2) and C (x_3, y_3), why the area of triangle ABC is

$\frac{1}{2}[x_1(y_2 - y_3) + x_2(y_3 - y_1) + x_3(y_1 - y_2)]$

Ans :

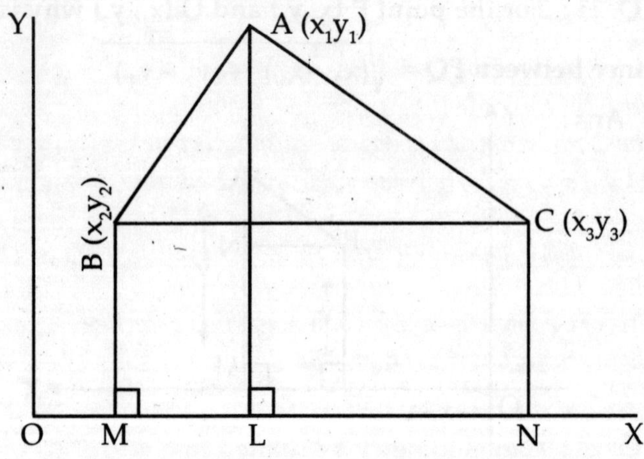

Draw AL, BM and CN perpendiculars from A, B, C on x–ax is ar (ABC) = ar (ABML) + ar (ALNC) – ar (BMNC)

$$=\frac{1}{2}(BM+AL)\times ML+\frac{1}{2}(AL+CN)\times LN-\frac{1}{2}(BM+CN)\times MN$$

$$=\frac{1}{2}\left[(y_2+y_1)(x_1-x_2)+\frac{1}{2}(y_1+y_3)(x_3-x_1)-\frac{1}{2}(y_2+y_3)(x_3-x_2)\right]$$

$$=\frac{1}{2}[x_1(y_2+y_1-y_1-y_3)+x_3(-y_2-y_1+y_2+y_3)]$$

$$+x_2(-y_2-y_1+y_2+y_3)$$

$$=\frac{1}{2}[x_1(y_2-y_3)+x_2(y_3-y_1)+x_3(y_1-y_2)]$$

Q. 23 : What is the origin of word 'Geometry'?

Ans : The word Geometry simply means measuring the land. Euclid is called the father of Geometry. He had written 13 volumes of geometry books called Elements.

D.E. Smith writes –

Euclid did not use the word geometry nor called his treatise geometry, probably because the term still related to land measure, but spoke of it merely as the elements. Indeed he did not employ the word 'Geometry' at all, although it was in common use among Greek writers. When Euclid was translated into Latin in the 12th century, the Greek title was changed to the Latin from Elementa, but the word, geometry is often found in the title–page, first page, or last page of the early printed editions. (D.E. Smith Vol. 2 Page 273)

Geometry appears in English in 14th century manuscripts. An anonymous 14th century manuscript begins," Nowe sues here a Tretis of Geometri where by you may knowe the heighte, depens and the brede of most what erthely thynges" (D.E. Smith Vol. 1 Page 237)

Q. 24 : Can Geometry be related to Nature?

Ans : Yes, Geometry can be well–related to nature.

The most common thing which you can find in nature is symmetry.

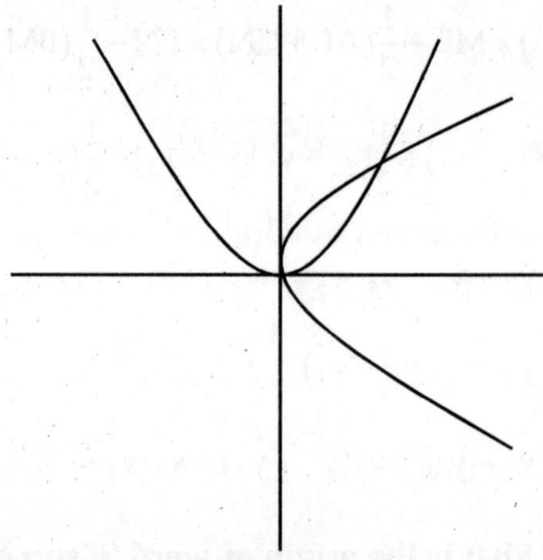

Symmetry means same shape around the axes. You can see your body is symmetrical.

(ii) A ball when hit by a batsman makes a parabolic shape.

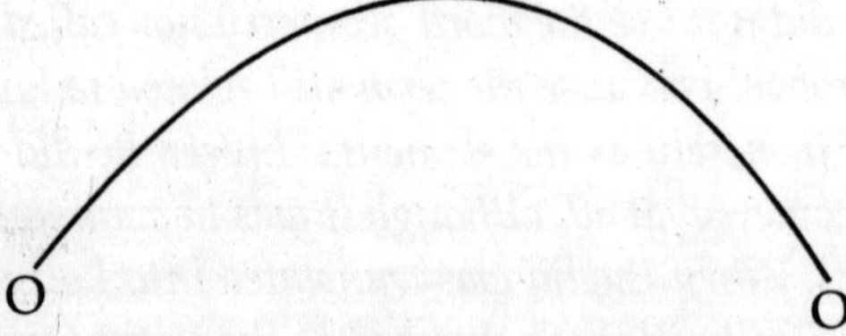

(iii) Some fruits such as apple, banana, pineapples exhibit fibonacci number.
(iv) The sun, the moon, the earth are all circular in shape.
(v) The light travels in a straight line.
(vi) The planet travels in elliptical path.
(vii) The spider's web is in the shape of logarithmic spiral.

❑

ALGEBRA

Q. 1 : For the given quadratic equation

$$ax^2 + bx + c = 0$$

why $x = \dfrac{-b \pm \sqrt{D}}{2a}$ **is taken?**

Ans : We know that the general form of a quadratic equation is $ax^2 + bx + c = 0$

Multiplying both sides by 4a, we get

$4a^2x^2 + 4abx + 4ac = 0$

$$\Rightarrow (2ax)^2 + 2.2ax.b + b^2 + 4ac - b^2 = 0$$

(Completing the square)

$$\Rightarrow [2ax + b]^2 = b^2 - 4ac$$

$$\Rightarrow 2ax + b = \pm\sqrt{b^2 - 4ac}$$

$$\Rightarrow 2ax = \frac{-b \pm \sqrt{b^2 - 4ac}}{2}$$

$$\Rightarrow x = \frac{-b \pm \sqrt{b^2 - 4ac}}{2a}$$

Where $b^2 - 4ac = D$

Hence, $x = \dfrac{-b \pm \sqrt{D}}{2a}$

This proof of extracting the roots of a quadratic polynomial was given by the Indian mathematician Sridhara.

If we consider the two roots of x as α and β

then $\alpha = \frac{-b+\sqrt{b^2-4ac}}{2a}$

and $\beta = \frac{-b-\sqrt{b^2-4ac}}{2a}$

(i) Hence, Sum of Roots $(\alpha+\beta) =$

$$\frac{-b+\sqrt{b^2-4ac}\,(+)-b-\sqrt{b^2-4ac}}{2a}$$

$$= \frac{-2b}{2a} = \frac{-b}{a}$$

(iii) Product of Roots $(\alpha\beta) =$

$$\left(\frac{-b+\sqrt{b^2-4ac}}{2a}\right) \times \left(\frac{-b-\sqrt{b^2-4ac}}{2a}\right)$$

$$= \frac{(-b)^2-(b^2-4ac)}{4a^2}$$

$$= \frac{b^2-b^2+4ac}{4a^2} = \frac{4ac}{4aa} = \frac{c}{a}$$

Q. 2 : Why log a^{mn} = log a^m + log a^n?

Ans : We know that if $a^x = N$

$\Rightarrow \log a^N = x$

Let us suppose,

$\log a^m = x$

$\Rightarrow a^x = m$

And $\log a^n = y$

$\Rightarrow a^y = n$

Hence,

$mn = a^x . a^y = a^{x+y}$

$\Rightarrow a^{x+y} = mn$

$\Rightarrow \log a^{mn} = x + y$

$= \log a^m + \log a^n$

Q. 3 : Why $\log a^{m/n} = \log a^m - \log a^n$?

Ans : Suppose $\log a^m = x \Rightarrow a^x = m$

$\log a^n = y \Rightarrow a^y = m$

Hence $\frac{m}{n} = \frac{a^x}{a^y} = a^{x-y}$

$= \log a^m - \log a^n$

Q. 4 : Why $\log a^1 = 0$?

Ans : Let $\log a^1 = x$

$\Rightarrow a^x = 1$

$\Rightarrow a^x = a^0$

$\Rightarrow x = 0$

$\Rightarrow \log a^1 = 0$

Q. 5 : Why $\log a^a = 1$?

Ans : Let $\log a^a = x$

$\Rightarrow a^x = a$

$\Rightarrow a^x = a^1$

$\Rightarrow x = 1$

$\Rightarrow \log a^a = 1$

Q. 6 : Why $a^{\log a^N} = N$

Ans : Let $\log a^N = N$

$$\Rightarrow a^x = N$$
$$\Rightarrow a^{\log_a N} = N$$

Q. 7 : Why $n_{p_r} = \dfrac{n!}{n-r!}$ For $0 \le r \le n$

Ans : We know that the number of permutations of n different objects taken r at a time, where $0 \le r \le n$ and the objects do not repeat is n (n–1) (n–2)............(n–r+1) which is denoted by n_{p_r}.

For fitting r vacant places by n objects is denoted by n_{p_r}.

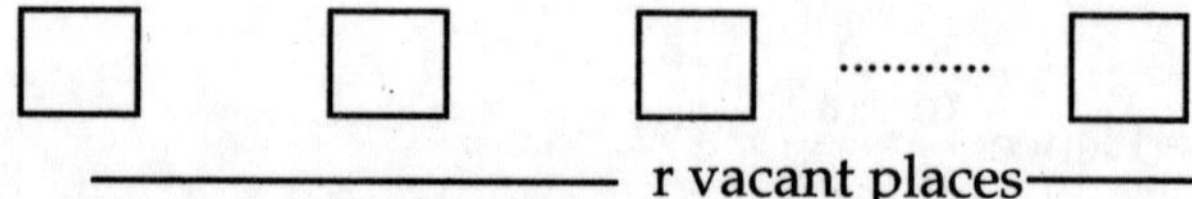

First place can be filled in n ways
Second place can be filled in (n–1) ways
Third place can be filled by (n–3) ways. Continuing the above ways, the number of ways of filling in r vacant places in succession is

n (n – 1) ...... [n – (r – 1)] ways.

i.e. $n_{p_r} = n(n-1)(n-2) \ldots\ldots (n-r+1)$

Multiplying and dividing by (n – r) (n – r – 1) ....2×1

$$n_{p_r} = \frac{n(n-1)\ldots\ldots(n-r+1)\{(n-r)(n-r-1)\ldots 2.1\}}{(n-r)(n-r-1)\ldots\ldots 2\times 1}$$

$$= \frac{n!}{n-r!} \text{ when } 0 < r \le n$$

Q. 8 : Why $n_{c_r} = \dfrac{n!}{r!\,n-r!}$?

Ans : Let the number of combinations of n distinct objects taken r at a time be x. Consider one of these x ways. There are r objects in this selection which can be arranged on r! ways. Thus, each of x combinations gives rise to r! permutations. So x combinations will give rise to $x \times r!$ permutations. Consequently, the number of permutations of n things, taken r at a time is $(x) \times r!$. But this number is also equal to n_{P_r}.

$$(x)\, r! = n_{P_r}$$

$$\Rightarrow x = \frac{n_{P_r}}{r!}$$

$$= \left(\frac{n!}{n - r!}\right) \times \frac{1}{r!}$$

$$= \frac{n!}{n - r!\, r!}$$

$$\Rightarrow n_{c_r} = \frac{n!}{r!\ \ n - r!}$$

$$= \frac{n(n-1)(n-2)(n-3).........3.2.1}{[r(r-1).......2.1][(n-r)(n-r-1)....2.1]}$$

Q. 9 : What is the difference between common logarithm and natural logarithm.

Ans : **Natural Logarithm :** In case of natural logarithm the base is taken as e where e lies between 2 and 3; and e

$$= 1 + \frac{1}{1!} + \frac{1}{2!} + \frac{1}{3!} + ...$$

Base	Symbol	Name
10	log	Common logarithm
e	ln	Natural logarithm

For theoretical verification, logarithm to the base e is called Napierian logarithms

$\log 10^{a} = \log a$ and

$\log e^{a} = \ln a$

Logarithm on the Napierian base can be converted into common logarithm by this relation

$\log e^{a} = \log 10^{a} . \log e^{10}$

or $\log 10^{a} = \dfrac{1}{\log e^{10}} \times \log e^{a}$

$= 0.434 . \log e^{a}$

(ii) Common Logarithm : Popularly known as Brigg's system it always takes base as 10. It is very useful in a practical calculations. If no base is written then the base is always considered as 10.

i.e. $\log 10 = \log 10^{10}$

Q. 10 : What is the difference between AP, GP and HP?

Ans :

AP (ARITHMETIC PROGRESSION)

A sequence, each term of which is equal to the sum of the preceding term and a constant. Example : 2, 5, 8, 11.......

If a = first term

d = common difference

Then the series will be–

a, a + d, a + 2d, a + 3d ....a + (n–1) d.

Here, a + (n–1) d = l_1 is the last or nth term S_n

$= \dfrac{n}{2}\{2a + (n-1)d\}$ = Sum to n terms

G P (GEOMETRIC PROGRESSION)

A sequence for which the ratio of a term to its predecessor is the same for all terms. a, ar, ar^2..........ar^{n-1} are the first n terms of GP.

Where r = Common ratio = $\dfrac{\text{second term}}{\text{first term}}$

Example 2, 4, 8, 16, 32..........

H P (HORMONIC PROGRESSION)

A sequence whose reciprocals form an arithmetic sequence is called Harmonic Progression.

Example : $1, \frac{1}{2}, \frac{1}{3}, \frac{1}{4} \ldots\ldots \frac{d}{n}$

are the first n terms of a Harmonic Progression.

Q. 11 : Why in an AP

$a_n = a + (n-1)\,d$ where a, n and d have the usual meaning.

Ans : In the previous question we have discussed about A.P. Let us think about the progress of a term.

a_2 = 2nd term = a + d
a_3 = 3rd term = a + d + d = a + 2d
a_4 = 4th term = a +2d + d = a + 3d
a_5 = 5th term = a + 3d + d = a + 4d

i.e. every next term is the sum of previous term and the common difference taken together.

Observe the above and see what conclusion can you draw from the above.

3rd term = $a + 2 \times d = a + (3-1)\,d$
4th term = $a + 3 \times d = a + (4-1)\,d$
5th term = $a + 4 \times d = a + (5-1)\,d$

In the same fashion,

nth term = $a + (n-1)\,d$

Hence $a_n = a + (n-1)\,d$

Q. 12 : Why $S_n = \frac{n}{2}\{2a + (n-1)d\}$

Ans : Let a, a + d, a + 2d, a + 3d.......a + (n –1) d be the first n terms of an A P.

$S_n = a + (a + d) + (a + 2d) + (a + 3d) + \ldots\ldots \{a + (n-1)\,d\}$..(I)
$S_n = \{a + (n-1)\,d\} + \{a + (n-2)\,d\} + \ldots\ldots\ldots\ldots + a\ldots\ldots\ldots\ldots$ (II)

[Reversing the order of (1)]

ADDING EQUATION (I) AND (II) WE GET

$$2S_n=\{2a+(n-1)d\}+\{2a+(n-1)\,d\} \overset{n \text{ times}}{+\ldots\ldots\ldots\ldots} +\{2a + (n-1)\,d\}$$

$$\Rightarrow 2S_n = n\{2a+(n-1)d\}$$

$$\Rightarrow S_n = \frac{n}{2}\{2a+(n-1)d\}$$

Q. 13 : Why $1^2 + 2^2 + 3^2 + ... + n^2 = \dfrac{n(n+1)(2n+1)}{6}$

Ans : We know that
$(k+1)^3 - k^3 = 3k^2 + 3k + 1$
Put K = 1, 2, 3.........n in the above expression.

$$2^3 - 1^3 = 3.1^2 + 3.1 + 1$$
$$3^3 - 2^3 = 3.2^2 + 3.2 + 1$$
$$4^3 - 3^3 = 3.3^2 + 3.3 + 1$$

$$(n+1)^3 - n^3 = 3.n^2 + 3.n + 1$$

Adding the above series, we get,
$(n+1)^3 - 1^3 = 3. (1^2 + 2^2 + 3^2 + .. + n^2) + 3 (1 + 2 + .. + n) + n$

$\Rightarrow n^3 + 3n^2 + 3n + 1 - 1 = 3 \sum n^2 + 3. \dfrac{n(n+1)}{2} + n$

[Using $(a+b)^3 = a^3 + 3a^2b + 3ab^2 + b^3$

and $1 + 2 + ... + n = \dfrac{n(n+1)}{2}$]

$$\Rightarrow n^3 + 3n^2 + 3n - \frac{3(n^2+n)}{2} - n = 3\sum n^2$$

$$\Rightarrow \frac{2n^3 + 6n^2 + 6n - 3n^2 - 3n - 2n}{2} = 3\sum n^2$$

$$\Rightarrow \frac{2n^3 + 3n^2 + n}{2 \times 3} = \sum n^2$$

$$\Rightarrow \frac{n(2n^2 + 3n + 1)}{6}$$

$$\Rightarrow \frac{n(2n^2 + 2n + n + 1)}{6} = \sum n^2$$

$$\Rightarrow \frac{n[2n(n+1) + 1(n+1)}{6} = \sum n^2$$

$$\Rightarrow \frac{n(2n+1)(n+1)}{6} = \Sigma n^2 = 1^2 + 2^2 + \ldots\ldots + n^2$$

Q. 14 : How can the general algebraic identities be derived?

Ans : The general algebraic identities such as

$$(a \pm b)^2 = a^2 \pm 2ab + b^2$$

$$(a \pm b)^3 = a^3 \pm 3a^2b + 3ab^2 \pm b^3$$

$$(a \pm b)^4 = a^4 \pm 4a^3b + ba^2 \pm 4a^1b^3 + b^4$$

can easily be derived by using Pascal Triangle.

PASCAL TRIANGLE

A triangular array of numbers composed of the coefficients in the expansion of $(x + y)^n$ for n = 0, 1, 2, 3....etc.

The triangle extends down infinitely, the coefficients in the expansion of $(x + y)^n$, being in the (n+1)th row.

The array described below is bordered by 1's and the sum of two adjacent numbers in one row is equal to the number in the next row between the two numbers. This array is symmetric about the vertical line through the vertex.

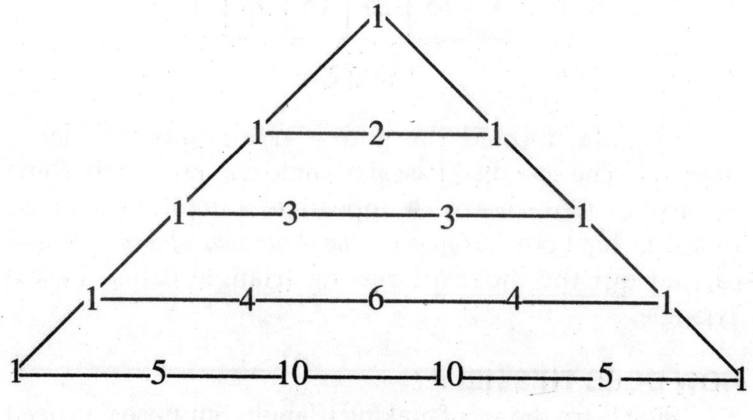

Table 1

Pingala, a writer in 3rd century BC, in his book *Chanda–Sastra* had described the following method, which is similar to the Pascal Triangle. Pingala writes—

"First draw a square, below it and starting from the middle of lower side, draw two squares on either side. Draw 3, 4, 5, squares below these. Write the number 1 in the middle of the top 8 square. Inside every other sqaure the number to be written is the sum of the numbers to be squares above it and overlapping it."

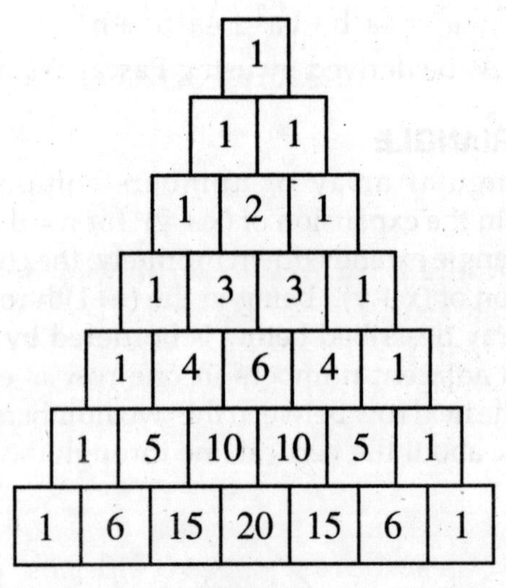

Table 2

Pingala, named the above arrangement *"Meru-Prastara"*. The so-called Pascal triangle was known in China as early as 1261. In 1261 it appears to a depth of 6. Blaise Pascal in his book *Treatise on the Arithmetical Triangle* had carried out the most interesting triangle called Pascal Triangle.

HOW DOES THIS HELP?

First learn the art of making triangle. Suppose you need to find the expansion of

(i) $(a + b)^3$

(ii) $(a + b)^5$
(iii) $(a - b)^4$

with the help of Pascal Triangle. You do the following and get the desired result in a few seconds.

(i) Move into the row which is equal to the power of expansion.

(ii) Note down the coefficients written there with certain gaps, with desired (+/–) sign.

(iii) Write the maximum power of 'a' and minimum power (0) of 'b' as first coefficient.

(iv) Keep increasing the power of 'b' and decreasing the power of 'a' until every coefficient is taken into consideration.

EXAMPLES

1. $(a + b)^3 = ?$

(i) Move the third row to write the coefficients of expansion; they are

1 3 3 1

(ii) Since you are to expand the binomial having (+) sign in between, let (+) sign take its place.

1 +3 +3 +1

(iii) Put the maximum power of 'a' (*i.e.* 3) and minimum power of b (*i.e.* 0) as the first part of coefficient.

(iv) Keep increasing the power of 'b' by 1 and decreasing the power of 'a' by 1.

$$= 1a^3b^\circ + 3a^2b^1 + 3a^1b^2 + 1.a^\circ b^3$$

$$= a^3 + 3a^2b + 3ab^2 + b^3 \; [\because a^\circ = 1, b^\circ = 1]$$

2. $(a + b)^5 = ?$

(i) Write the value expressed in 5th row of table with (+) sign.

1 +5 +10 +10 +5 +1

(ii) Place the power of 'a' and 'b' accordingly.

$$= 1a^5b^\circ + 5a^4b^1 + 10a^3b^2 + 10a^2b^3 + 5a^1b^4 + 1a^\circ b^4$$

$= a^5 + 5a^4b + 10a^3b^2 + 10a^ab^3 + 5ab^4 + b^4$

3. $(a - b)^4 = ?$

(i) Write the value of coefficients expressed in 4th row of table.

(ii) When there is a negative sign in the binomial expansion, put (+) and (–) sign alternatively.

$= 1 \quad -4 \quad +6 \quad -4 \quad +1$

(iii) Place the power of 'a' and 'b' accordingly.

$(a - b)^4 = 1a^4b^\circ - 4a^3b^1 + 6a^2b^2 - 4a^1b^3 + 1a^\circ b^4$

$= a^4 - 4a^3b + 6a^2b^2 - 4ab^3 + b^4$

Q. 15 : Is zero a multiple of every number ?

Ans : Different books put different opinions regarding zero being the multiple of any number but once you go through the reasoning discussed here, you will certainly accept that zero is a multiple of every number.

Let x and y be integers. Then x is a multiple of y if there exists another integer z such that

$x = y \times z$

Suppose $x = 0$ and let y be an arbitrary integer, then to be $x = 0$, z must be zero. So zero is a multiple of every integer.

Q. 16 : Why

$$1^3 + 2^3 + \ldots\ldots\ldots\ldots + n^3 = \frac{n^2(n+1)^2}{4} = \left(\frac{n\,(n+1)}{2}\right)^2 = (\Sigma n)^2 ?$$

Ans : We know that,

$$(k+1)^4 - k^4 = 4k^3 + 6k^2 + 4k + 1$$

Put k = 1, 2, 3..............n in the above expression.

$$2^4 - 1^4 = 4.1^3 + 6.1^2 + 4.1 + 1$$
$$3^4 - 2^4 = 4.2^3 + 6.2^2 + 4.2 + 1$$
$$4^4 - 3^4 = 4.3^3 + 6.3^2 + 4.3 + 1$$
- -
$$(n+1)^4 - n^4 = 4.n^3 + 6n^2 + 4n + 1$$

Adding we get,

$(n + 1)^4 - n^4 = 4\,(1^3 + 2^3 + . + n^3) + 6\,(1^2 + 2^2 +.+n^2) + 4\,(1 + 2 + . + n)$

$$\Rightarrow n^4 + 4n^3 + 6n^2 + 4n = 4\sum n^3 + 4\sum n + n$$

$$\Rightarrow n^4 + 4n^3 + 6n^2 + 4n - 6\sum n^2 - 4\sum n - n = 4\sum n^3$$

$$\Rightarrow n^4 + 4n^3 + 6n^2 + 4n - \frac{6n(n+1)(2n+1)}{6} - \frac{4^2.n(n+1)}{2} - n$$

$$= 4\sum n^3$$

$$\Rightarrow 4\sum n^3 = n^4 + 4n^3 + 6n^2 + 4n - n\,(2n^2 + 3n + 1) - 2n^2$$

$$-2n-n$$

$=n^4 + 4n^3 + 6n^2 + 4n - 2n^3 - 3n^2 - n - 2n^2 - 3n$

$= n^4 + 2n^3 + n^2$

$= n^2\,(n^2 + 2n + 1)$

$= n^2\,(n + 1)^2$

$$\Rightarrow \sum n^3 = \frac{n^2(n+1)^2}{4}$$

$$= \left[\frac{n\,(n+1)}{2}\right]^2$$

$$= \left[\sum n\right]^2$$

$$\Rightarrow 1^3 + 2^3 + - - + n^3 = \left[\sum n\right]^2$$

Q. 17 : Why 1+2+3+...............+ n = $\frac{n(n+1)}{2}$?

Ans : This is a simple generalisation of sum to n terms of an AP.

Let a and d be the first term and common difference of an AP.

Here a = 1, d = 2 – 1 = 1 and n = m

Applying the formula for S_n in an AP series

$$S_n = \frac{n}{2}\{2a + (n-1)d\}$$

$$= \frac{n}{2}\{2 \times 1 + (n-1) \times 1\}$$

$$= \frac{n}{2}\{2 + n - 1\}$$

$$= \frac{n}{2}\{n + 1\}$$

$$= \frac{n(n+1)}{2}$$

Q. 18 : What do you mean by infinity in Mathematics?

Ans : Infinity respresents a symbol for a value that is so large that we cannot imagine it. No matter what number you take, it will always be less than infinity.

Aristotle is true when he says—"Only a finite number of natural numbers has ever been written down or has ever been conceived. If L is the largest number conceived up till now then I will go further and write down L + 1 or $L^2 + 1$ but still only finitely many have been conceived."

Bhaskaracharya in his famous book *Lilavati* writes— *"Kh Bhajito Rashi Khahar syat"*

(खः भाजितो राशिः खहर स्यात्)

i.e. any number divided by zero is called *khahar*. He further adds—

"In the quantity consisting of that which has zero for its divisor, there is no alteration, though many may be inserted or extracted; as no change takes place in the infinite and immutable God when worlds are created or destroyed though numerous orders of beings are observed or put forth."

$$\frac{a}{0} = \infty$$

$\infty - 0 = \infty$

$\infty + 0 = \infty$

The present symbol of infinity is due to the English mathematician John Wallis, who was born in England on Nov. 23, 1616 and died on Oct. 28, 1703.

Q. 19 : Which one is larger n^n or $(n+1)^{n-1}$

Ans : The answer to this problem can be established by the given example.

n	n^n	$(n+1)^{n-1}$
2	4	3
3	27	16
4	256	125
5	3125	1296
6	46656	16807

What conclusion can you draw from the above?

The above expansion clearly shows that n^n grows faster than $(n+1)^{n-1}$.

Q. 20 : If $a > b$ then why $-a < -b$?

Ans : We have, $a > b$

Subtract a from both the sides

$a - a > b - a$

$0 > b - a$

Now subtract b from both sides.

$0 - b > b - a - b$

$\Rightarrow -b > -a$

$\Rightarrow -a < -b$

I hope this example will help you to understand, why $20 > -24$ changes to $20 < 24$.

Q. 21 : How to add and subtract two inequalities, say $a > b$ and $c < d$?

Ans : Adding two inequalities is as simple as adding

two numbers, but what you need to keep in mind is that the sign of both the inequalities should move in the same direction.

Example : Add $5 > 4$ and $1 < 3$

$$\begin{array}{r} 5 > 4 \\ +3 > 1 \\ \hline 8 > 5 \\ \hline \end{array} \quad [(3>1) \text{ Change the result } 1 < 3]$$

Example : Subtract $5 > 4$ and $1 < 3$?

$$\begin{array}{rr} 5 > 4 \Rightarrow & 5 > 4 \\ 1 < 3 \Rightarrow & \underline{-1 > -3} \\ & 4 > 1 \\ \hline \end{array}$$

Q. 22 : Why $(-a) \times (+b) = -ab$?

Ans : This can be proved algebraically, very easily.

For $a, b > 0$

Consider, $0 \times b = 0$

$$\Rightarrow [a + (-a)] \times b = 0$$

$$\Rightarrow a \times b + (-a) \times b = 0 \quad \text{(by Distributive law)}$$

$$\Rightarrow (-a) \times b = 0 - a \times b$$

$$= -ab$$

$$\Rightarrow (-a) \times (b) = -ab$$

Q. 23 : Why $(-a)^0 = 1$ but $-a^0 = -1$?

Ans : The algebraic proof of any number raised to the power zero is 1 is known to all. A proof of ($a^0 = 1$) is also given in this book.

The basic difference between

$-a^0$, $(-a)^0$ and $(-a^0)$ is only the parenthesis which differentiates the final result. Let us understand the concept with example.

$$4^3 = 4 \times 4 \times 4 = 64$$

$$-4^3 = -(4 \times 4 \times 4) = -64$$

$$(-4)^3 = -4 \times -4 \times -4 = -64$$

Now, let us return to the original problem, we know $(a)^0 = 1$, so as $(-a)^0 = 1$

Now take the case of $-a^0$.

$-a^0 = -(a)^0 = -1$

This is also similar to $(-a)^0 = 1$

Q. 24 : Why $\frac{a}{b} = \frac{c}{d} \Rightarrow ad = bc$?

Ans : If $\frac{a}{b} = \frac{c}{d}$

$\Rightarrow ad = bc$

This method is known as **cross–multiplication method.** Now the problem is why do you cross-multiply?

When you cross–multiply, you are doing nothing except that you are multiplying both the sides by the same fractional number say $\left(\frac{x}{x}\right)$.

If $\frac{a}{b} = \frac{c}{d}$

$\Rightarrow \frac{a}{b} \times \frac{d}{d} = \frac{c}{d} \times \frac{b}{b}$

$\Rightarrow \frac{ad}{bd} = \frac{cb}{db}$

Since denominators of both the sides are same, Hence they will get cancelled out.

$\Rightarrow \frac{ad}{bd} = \frac{bc}{bd}$

$\Rightarrow ad = bc$

i.e. $\frac{a}{b} = \frac{c}{d}$

$$= \frac{a}{b} \times \frac{c}{d}$$

$$\Rightarrow ad = bc$$

Q. 25 : What is a Golden Triangle?

Ans : A Golden triangle is an isosceles triangle in which two longer sides have equal lengths and in which the ratio of this length to that of the third, smaller side is the golden ratio.

$$\phi = \frac{1+\sqrt{5}}{2}$$

Q. 26 : What is a Googol?

Ans : A googol is the number which you get when 1 is followed by 100 zeros.

This is too big to imagine. It is astonishing to know that there are fewer atoms than a googol in universe. The googol was invented by the American mathematician Edward Kasner (1878–1955). According to the story, Kasner asked his nephew Milton Sirotta, who was 8 years old then to suggest a name for the big number he had discovered. To this Sirotta replied "Googol".

Googol = 10^{100}

1 googol = 10000000000, 0000000000, 0000000000, 0000000000, 0000000000, 0000000000, 0000000000, 0000000000, 0000000000,0000000000

Q. 27 : What is a googolplex?

Ans : A googolplex is the largest number so far mathematicians have discovered. It is larger than the number of atoms present on the Earth.

A googolplex is a 1 with a googol zeros behind it. In other words, a googolplex is 1 with 10^{100} zeros.

1 googolplex = $10^{10^{100}}$

Let us look at the scientific notation of some of the numbers and estimate how big a googolplex is?

Thousand – 10^3

Million – 10^6
Thousand Million – 10^9
Billion – 10^{12}
Thousand Billion – 10^{15}
Trillion – 10^{18}
Imagine how big a googolplex is?

Q. 28 : What is the difference between Monomial, Binomial and Polynomial?

Ans : Let us take each term separately.

MONOMIAL

An algebraic expression consisting of a single term which is a product of numbers and variables.

Example : 3x, $6x^2$.......etc.

BINOMIAL

An algebraic expression consisting of two terms such as 2x + 5y, 3x – 4z.........etc.

TRINOMIAL

An algebraic expression consisting of three terms such as 4x + 5y + 3z, $x^2 - 3x + 2$......etc.

POLYNOMIAL

A polynomial in one variable (usually called simply a polynomial) of degree n is a rational integeral algebraic expression in the form of :

$$a_0x^n + a_1x^{n-1} + a_2x^{n-2} + \ldots\ldots + a_nx^o$$

Where a_i, i = 0, 1, 2........n, are complex numbers (real or imaginary) and n is a non–negative integer.

A polynomial may be further classified as – linear, quadratic, cubic, quartic (or biquadratic), quantic etc, according to the degree of the variable.

General Equation	*Name*	*Degree*
$ax^1 + by^1$	Linear	1
$ax^2 + bx + c$	Quadratic	2

$ax^3 + bx^2 + cx + d$	Cubic	3
$ax^4 + bx^3 + cx^2 + dx + e$	Quartic	4
$ax^5 + bx^4 + cx^3 + dx^2 + ex + f$	Quantic	5

Q. 29 : What is HCF, LCM and LCD?

Ans : **HCF :** The Highest Common Factor (HCF) or GCD (Greatest Common Divisior) or GCM (Greatest Common Multiple) of two numbers of more than two numbers is the greatest number which divides each one of them exactly.

Example : Find the HCF of 12 and 16.

All factors of 12 = 1, 2, 3, 4, 6 and 12

All factors of 16 = 1, 2, 4, 8 and 16.

Common factor = 1, 2, 4

Highest Common factor = 4

Hence HCF of (12, 16) = 4

RULE FOR FINDING HCF

Suppose you are given two numbers. Divide the larger number by the smaller one. Now divide the divisor by the remainder. Go on dividing the preceding divisor by the remainder last obtained, till a remainder 0 is obtained. The last divisor obtained is the required HCF of two given numbers.

In case more than two numbers are given, then choose any two numbers and find their HCF. The HCF of these two numbers and third number, gives the HCF of these three numbers and so on.

Example : Find the HCF of 777 and 1147

Solution : 777) 1147(1
–777
370) 777(2
–740
37) 370 (10
–370
X

Hence HCF of (777, 1147) = 37

Example : Find the HCF of 20, 24 and 36

Solution :

```
20) 24 (1
   -20
   ----
    4) 20 (5
      -20
      ----
        X
      ----
```

Now HCF, (20, 24) = 4

Now find the HCF of 4 and 36.

```
4) 36 (9
  -36
  ----
    X
  ----
```

Hence HCF of (20, 24, 36) = 4

LCM

The least number which is exactly divisible by each one of the given numbers is called their LCM.

Example : Find the LCM of 12 and 18

Solution : Multipes of 12 are—

12, 24, 36, 48, 60, 72, 84.........

Multiples of 18 are—

18, 36, 54, 72, 90, 108........

Common Multiples are —

12, 36, 72........

Least Common Multiple = 36

Hence LCM of (12, 18) = 36

Example : Find LCM of 12, 15 and 18

Solution :

2	12 –	15 –	18
3	6 –	15 –	19
	2 –	5 –	3

LCM = 2 × 3 × 2 × 5 × 3 = 180

LCD

LCD or Least Common Divisor of two or more fractions is a common multiple of the denominations.

LCD tells us to equalise the denominator of fractional terms before doing the addition or subaction. Suppose we have to add $\frac{1}{2}$ and $\frac{1}{3}$. First make the denominator of these terms equal. This can be done by multiplying $\frac{1}{2}$ to $\frac{3}{3}$ and $\frac{1}{3}$ to $\frac{2}{2}$

$$\frac{1}{2} = \frac{1}{2} \times \frac{3}{3} = \frac{3}{6}$$

$$\frac{1}{3} = \frac{1}{3} \times \frac{2}{2} = \frac{2}{6}$$

LCD helps in adding or subtracting the fraction.

Q. 30 : Prove that Product of two numbers = HCF × LCM.

Ans : Let a and b be two given numbers. Let their HCF and LCM be x and y. On dividing a and b by x, let the quotient be m and n resprectively.

$\Rightarrow a = mx$ and $b = nx$

Hence the LCM of a and b = mnx

But the LCM, as supposed at the beginning = y
$\Rightarrow y = mnx$

Now $a \times b = mx \times nx$

$= mnx^2$

$= mnx \times x$

$= y \times x$

Hence $a \times b = y \times x$

Product of two numbers = LCM × HCF

Q. 31 : Prove $n_{c_r} + n_{c_{r-1}} = n+1_{c_r}$

Such that $r \le n$

Ans : $n_{c_r} + n_{c_{r-1}} = \dfrac{n!}{(n-r)!r!} + \dfrac{n!}{(n-r+1)!(r-1)!}$

$$= \frac{n!}{(n-r)!.r.(r-1)!} + \frac{n!}{(n-r+1).(n-r)!.(r-1)!}$$

$$= \frac{n!}{(n-r)!(r-1)!}\left[\frac{1}{r} + \frac{1}{n-r+1}\right]$$

$$= \frac{n!}{(n-r)!(r-1)!}\left[\frac{n-\not{r}+1+\not{r}}{r(n-r+1)}\right]$$

$$= \frac{n!.(n+1)}{(n-r)!.(r-1)!.r(n-r+1)}$$

$$= \frac{(n+1).n!}{[(n-r+1).(n-r)!]\times[r.(r-1)!]}$$

$$= \frac{(n+1)!}{(n-r+1)!.r!}$$

[Here (n – r +1) (n –r)! = (n – r + 1)! and r (r –1)! = r!

Q. 32 : If $n_{c_x} = n_{c_y} \Rightarrow x = y \text{ or } x + y = n$, why?

Ans : We have $n_{c_x} = n_{c_y}$

$\Rightarrow n_{c_x} = n_{c_y} = n_{c_{n-y}}$ $[\because n_{c_y} = n_{c_{n-y}}]$

For $n_{c_x} = n_{c_y}$

$\Rightarrow x = y$

and if $n_{c_y} = nc_{n-y}$

$\Rightarrow x = n - y$

$\Rightarrow x + y = n$

Remember if $x \ne y$ then x + y = n

Q. 33 : Prove for $0 \le r \le n, n_{c_r} = n_{c_{n-r}}$

Ans : $n_{c_{n-r}} = \dfrac{n!}{(n-r)![n-(n-r)]!}$

$= \dfrac{n!}{(n-r)!(n-n+r)!}$

$= \dfrac{n!}{(n-r)!r!}$

$= n_{c_r}$

Q. 34 : Solve $\sqrt{x} + y = 11$ and $\sqrt{y} + x = 7$?

Ans : This is an interesting mathematical puzzle that is very difficult to solve. Here I shall discuss the three possible methods to solve this equation.

First Method : Graphical Method

For equation $\sqrt{x} + y = 11$

Put $x = 0, \Rightarrow y = 11$

$x = 4 \Rightarrow y = 9$

$x = 9 \Rightarrow y = 8$

$x = 16 \Rightarrow y = 7$

x	0	4	9	16
y	11	9	8	7

For equation $x + \sqrt{y} = 7$

Put $y = 0 \Rightarrow x = 7$

$y = 4 \Rightarrow x = 5$

$y = 9 \Rightarrow x = 4$

$y = 16 \Rightarrow x = 3$

Y	0	4	9	16
X	7	5	4	3

Plot the points on a graph sheet, and find the point of intersection. This point of intersection will give the solution to the given equations.

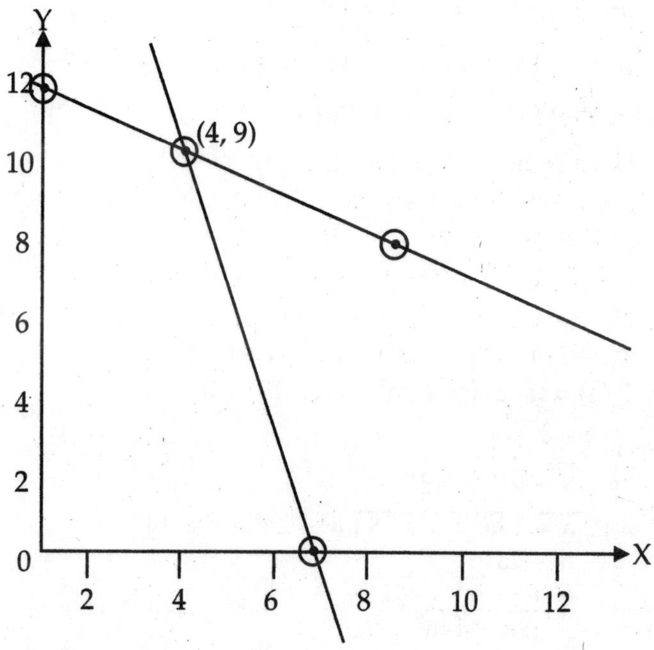

Point of intersection $\left.\begin{matrix} x = 4 \\ y = 9 \end{matrix}\right\}$

is the solution.

Second Method : Factor Method

If (x–a) is a factor of the polynomial P (x) then P (a) = 0

We have $\sqrt{x} + y = 11 - (1)$

$\sqrt{y} + x = 7 - (2)$

(2) $\Rightarrow \sqrt{y} = 7 - x$

$\Rightarrow y = (7-x)^2 = 49 - 14x + x^2$

Put the value of y in equation (1)

We have $\sqrt{x} + y = 11$

$\Rightarrow \sqrt{x} + x^2 - 14x + 49 = 11$

$\Rightarrow x^2 - 14x + \sqrt{x} + 49 - 11 = 0$

$\Rightarrow a^4 - 14a^2 + a + 38 = 0$ Put $x = a^2$

Here 38 has the factors 1, 2 and 19

$P(a) = a^4 - 14a^2 + a + 38$

$P(2) = 2^4 - 14(2)^2 + 2 + 38$

$= 16 - 56 + 2 + 38 = 0$

Hence a–2 is the factor of the polynomial P (a). Let us find the other factor of P (a) by division method.

$P(a) = (a-2)(a^3 + 2a^2 - 10a - 19) = 0$

$\Rightarrow a = 2$

i.e. $\sqrt{x} = 2 \Rightarrow x = 4$

$$
\begin{array}{l}
a-2)\overline{a^4 - 14a^2 + a + 38}\,(\,a^3 + 2a^2 - 10a - 19 \\
\quad a^4 - 2a^3 \\
\quad \underline{- \quad +} \\
\qquad 2a^3 - 14a^2 \\
\qquad \underline{-2a^3 \mp 4a^2} \\
\qquad - 10a^2 + a \\
\qquad - 10a^2 + 20a \\
\qquad \underline{+ \qquad -} \\
\qquad\quad -19a + 38 \\
\qquad\quad \underline{\mp 19a \pm 38} \\
\qquad\qquad \underline{0}
\end{array}
$$

For $x = 4, \Rightarrow y = 9$

Third Method :

$\sqrt{x}+y=11-(1)$

$\sqrt{y}+x=7-(2)$

Put $\sqrt{x}=9 \Rightarrow x=a^2$

$(1) \Rightarrow y=11-\sqrt{x}=11-a$

$\Rightarrow y^2=(11-a)^2$

$=121-22a+a^2-(3)$

Now, from equation (2), we have

$\sqrt{y}=7-x$

$\Rightarrow y=(7-x)^2=49-14x+x^2$

$=a^4-14a^2+49$

$\Rightarrow y^2=a^8+196a^4+2401-1372a^4-28a^6+98a^4—(4)$

Equating (3) and (4) we get,

$a^8-28a^6+294a^4-1373a^2+22a+2280=0—(5)$

For the above equation (5), Put a = 2

P (2) = 256 – 1792 + 4704 – 5492 + 44 + 2280

= 0

Hence a = 2

$\sqrt{x}=2$

$\Rightarrow x=4$

Put x = 4 in equation (1), we get

y + 2 = 11

$\Rightarrow y=9$

Hence the solution is x = 4, y = 9.

Q. 35 : The square root of 16 is 4, *i.e.* $\sqrt{16}=4$ and 16>4

But $\sqrt{0.16}=0.4$ and $0.16<0.4$. Why?

Ans : A decimal number has two parts.

(a) Whole Part (b) Fractional Part

The place value of every digit of whole part (from right to left) is 10 times the preceding number.

$238 = 2 \times 10^2 + 3 \times 10^1 + 8$

Whereas in fractional part, every next digit (from left to right) is $\frac{1}{10}$ times less than the previous one.

$$0.478 = \frac{4}{10} + \frac{7}{10^2} + \frac{8}{10^3}$$

$$\frac{4}{10} < \frac{7}{100} < \frac{8}{1000}$$

Now let us return to the original problem. Take some examples for generalisation of this problem.

$\sqrt{625} = 25$

$\sqrt{1225} = 35$

$\sqrt{2401} = 49$ etc.

In all the above, you notice that, the square root of the whole number always comes less than the original number. Had this not been the case, the concept that if

$a^1 = x \times x$

$\Rightarrow \sqrt{a} = x$

would come to a halt.

So, what conclusion do you get from the above? The square root of whole part comes to be less than the number, because if the place value of every digit of a number increases with the change of its place, the square root is likely to come smaller. Now take the case of fractional part where the place value of decimal part decreases with each successive digit, its square root is likely to come greater than the digit.

The inference which can be drawn from the above extract is that, when the place value of digit increases, its square root is less than the number, whose square root needs to be extracted and in the case of fractional part where the place value of each successive digit is $\frac{1}{10}$ times less than the previous one, its square root comes to be greater than the number.

Q. 36 : Name the mathematicians who have contributed in developing the mathematical symbols?

Ans : The journey of mathematical symbols began since the origin of the science of mathematics. There were hundreds of mathematicians who contributed to the development of mathematics and due to necessity to express mathematical languages they developed symbols. Here is a list of mathematical symbols and the names of mathematicians who finally contributed in its developement.

Symbols	Name	Date	Discoverer
+/−	Plus/Minus	1489	J. Widmann
×	Multiplication	1628	W. Oughtered
÷	Division	1659	Johann Rahn
%	Percentage	1425	Anonymous Italian Manuscript
√	Square Root	1525	Christoff Rudolf
$\sqrt{}$	Square Root	1637	Rene Descartes
Σ	Sigma	1755	Euler
π	Pi	1706	William Jones
∞	Infinity	1655	John Wallis
=	Equals to	1557	Robert Recorde
>/<	Greater than/ Less than	1631	Thomas Harriot
≤ / ≥	Greater than or equal to/ Less than or equal to	1734	Pierre Bouguer
p/q	Fraction	Around 1200	Fibonacci

:|::	Ratio/ Proportion	1897	G. Peano
i	Imaginary Quantity	1977	Euler
.	Decimal	1608	Simon Stevin
∠	Angle	1634	Pierre Herigone
⊥	Perpendicular	1634	Pierre Herigone
||	Parallel	1677	William Oughtered
Δ	Triangle	150 AD	Heron
≈	Congruence	1824	Karl Brandan Mollweidi
~	Similarity	1679	Leibniz
°	Degree	1571	Erasmus Reinhold
∩\∪	Intersection/ Union	1888	G. Peano
( )	Parenthesis	1663	G. Cardan
{ }	Braces	1593	F. Vieta
[ ]	Capital Bracket	1550	Rafael Bombelli
±	Plus or Minus	1631	William Oughtered
∟	Right Angle	Around 300 AD	Pappus
∴	Therefore	1659	Johann Rahn
f (x)	Function	1734	L. Euler
Π	Product Symbol	1812	Gauss
[x]	Greatest Integer	1962	Kenneth E Iverson

Q. 37 : Consider this example :

$$\begin{array}{r} 4\ \ 12\ \ 14 \\ -\,1\ \ \ 8\ \ \ 5 \\ \hline 3\ \ \ 4\ \ \ 9 \\ \hline \end{array}$$

Why do we take carry/borrow from the preceding digit of minuend when the digit at the same place in subtrahend is greater than the digit at minuend.

Ans : The process of subtraction can be understood by

decomposition method. Let us first understand the basics of subtraction.

$$\begin{array}{rl} 5\ 3\ 4 & \text{——— Minuend} \\ -1\ 8\ 5 & \text{——— Subtrahend} \\ \hline 3\ 4\ 9 & \text{——— Remainder} \\ \hline \end{array}$$

Since 4 > 5 and 3 > 8, so subtraction cannot be proceded, hence we need to understand the concept of subtraction.

$$\begin{array}{rcl} 534 & = & 500 + 30 + 4 \\ -185 & = & -(100 + 80 + 5) \\ \hline & = & (400 + 100) + (20 + 10) + 4 \\ & - & 100 \qquad \pm 80 \qquad + 5 \\ \hline & = & 400 + (100+20) + (10 + 4) \\ & - & 100 \pm 80 \pm 5 \\ \hline & = & 400 + 120 + 14 \\ & - & 100 \pm 80 \pm 5 \\ \hline & = & 300 + 40 + 9 \\ & = & 349 \end{array}$$

The concept of subtraction can be understood by method of equal addition.

$$\begin{array}{rcl} 534 & = & 500 + 30 + 4 \\ -185 & = & -100 + 80 + 5 \\ \hline \end{array}$$

Adding 110 on both the sides

$$\begin{array}{rl} = & 500 + (100 + 30) + (10 + 4) \\ - & 100 \pm (100 + 80) \pm (10+ 5) \\ \hline = & 500 + 130 + 14 \\ - & (100 +100) \pm (80 + 10) \pm 5 \\ \hline = & 500 + 130 + 14 \\ - & 200 \pm 90 \pm 5 \\ \hline = & 300 + 40 + 9 \\ = & 349 \end{array}$$

Q. 38 : Consider the given examples.

$$\begin{array}{r} 345 \\ \times 256 \\ \hline 2070 \\ 1725\times \\ +690\times\times \\ \hline 88320 \end{array}$$

Why do we put cross mark after each step of multiplication?

Ans : The basic logic of putting cross (X) lies in the process itself. Once the multiplication of unit digit is over, we put a cross mark below it and move to find the product of ten's digit. Once the multiplication of ten's digit is over, we put a cross mark below the ten's digit and move to find the product of next digit place at hundred position. This process continues till the product of every digit of multiplier has been placed. Let us understand the basic structure of 256, the multiplier. In place value system, 256 can be explicitly written as

$256 = 2 \times 100 + 5 \times 1 + 6$

Now look at the above example. You will find that 5 of 256 is at the ten's place. Hence a cross mark is placed below the unit place and the final product of 345 × 5 begins from the ten's place. Similarly 2 of 256 is at hundred place and so is its product written from the hundred place and hence two cross marks one below the unit place and another below the tens place are made.

Q. 39 : The Fundamental Theorem of Algebra states— "Every Polynomial of nth degree has n roots."

Suppose $x^3 = 1$, then certainly it should have three roots. x = 1 is obviously one root, then what are the other two roots?

Ans : Let $x^3 = 1$

$\Rightarrow x^3 - 1 = 0$

$\Rightarrow x^3 - 1^3 = 0$

$\Rightarrow (x-1)(x^2+x+1)=0 \; [a^3-b^3=(a-b)(a^2+ab+b^2)]$

$\Rightarrow$ Either $x-1=0$ or $x^2+x+1=0$

if $x-1=0 \Rightarrow x=1$

if $x^2+x+1=0$

$$\Rightarrow x = \frac{-1 \pm \sqrt{(1)^2 - 4 \times 1 \times 1}}{2}$$

$$= \frac{-1 + \sqrt{-3}}{2}$$

$$= \frac{-1 \pm \sqrt{-3i^2}}{2} \quad [\text{where } i^2 = -1]$$

$$= \frac{-1 \pm i\sqrt{3}}{2}$$

$$= \frac{-1 + i\sqrt{3}}{2} \text{ or } \frac{-1 - i\sqrt{3}}{2}$$

Hence, the three roots of 1 are

$$1, \frac{-1 + i\sqrt{3}}{2} \text{ and } \frac{-1 - i\sqrt{3}}{2}$$

Q. 40 : Consider the given question :

(a)
```
12) 365 (30
    -36
    ---
     ×5
    ---
```

(b)
```
12) 3612 (301
    -36
    ---
     ×12
     -12
     ---
       ×
     ---
```

In the case (a) one zero (0) has been put at the end making the quotient 30, whereas in example (b) zero (0)

has been placed after 3, making the quotient 301. What is the basis behind putting zeros in division?

Ans : Let us take the example given in case (1)

12) 365 (

Here Dividend = 365

Divisor = 12

```
12) 365 (3
    -36——  12 multiplied by 3
    × 5 ——  the next digit is carried down
```

Whenever you have the similar case, put zero, because the digit being carried out is less than the divisor. Let us understand it more explicitly.

```
12 ) 365 (30
    -360———12 times 30
       5
```

Let us take a similar problem

```
12 ) 395 (30
    -360———12 times 30
      35
```

Here 12 is multiplied by 30 times. Now the next step is to divide 35 by 12. Twice 12 is 24.

```
      2
     30
12) 395 (
    -360 ——12 times 30
      35
     -24——12 times 2
      11
```

Since we can't fit 12 into 11 any number of times, so we are done. All that remains is to add up the multiples of 12.

$395 = 30 \times 12 + 2 \times\ 12 \times +11$

$395 = (30 + 2) \times 12 + 11$

$395 = 32 \times 12 + 11$

Remainder

Divisor

Quotient

Dividend

Let us take another case :

12) 3612 (

We start with 300 times 12, to get 3600

```
        300
12)  3612 (
    –3600 ———— 12 times 300
       12
     – 12 ———— 12 times 1
        x
```

So, we have

$3612 = 300 \times 12 + 1 \times 12 + 0$

$3612 = (300 + 1) \times 12 + 0$

$3612 = 301 \times 12 + 0$

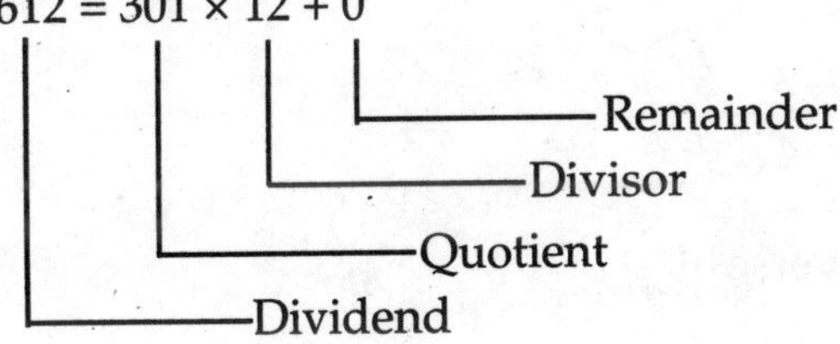

Q. 41 : In dividing a fraction

$\frac{a}{b} \div \frac{c}{d}$

Why do we write $\frac{a}{b} \div \frac{c}{d} = \frac{a}{b} \times \frac{d}{c}$ **?**

Ans : Division is the reverse process of multiplication.

$$a \div b = \frac{a}{b} = a \times \frac{1}{b}$$

What conclusion can you draw from it?
The conclusion is that if you are to divide any number x by another number say y, simply multiply x by $\frac{1}{y}$

Example : $4 \div 2 = 4 \times \frac{1}{2}$

Extend the case

$$a \div \frac{b}{c} = a \times (\text{inverse of } \frac{b}{c})$$

$$= a \times \frac{c}{b}$$

Now extend a step further

$$\frac{a}{b} \div \frac{c}{d} = \frac{a}{b} \times (\text{inverse of} \frac{c}{d})$$

$$= = \frac{a}{b} \times \frac{d}{c}$$

Example : $\frac{3}{4} \div \frac{5}{7}$

$$= \frac{3}{4} \times (\text{inverse of} \frac{5}{7})$$

$$= \frac{3}{4} \times \frac{7}{5}$$

Always remember, the multiplication inverse of x is $\frac{1}{x}$, because 1 is the multiplicative identity.

Q. 42 : Why $0 \le P(A) \le 1$

i.e. probability of a number lies between 0 and 1?

Ans : If there are n elementary events associated with a random experiment and m of them are favourable to an event A, then the probability of happening or occurance of event A is denoted by P (A) and is defined as the ratio $\frac{m}{n}$.

Thus, $P(A) = \frac{m}{n}$

Clearly, $o \leq m \leq n$

$\Rightarrow \frac{o}{m} \leq \frac{m}{n} \leq \frac{n}{n}$ [Dividing by n]

$\Rightarrow o \leq \frac{m}{n} \leq 1$

$\Rightarrow o \leq P(A) \leq 1$

Q. 43 : A rectangle has a side 3m and another 4m. Is its area 12 meters squared or 12 square metres.

Ans :

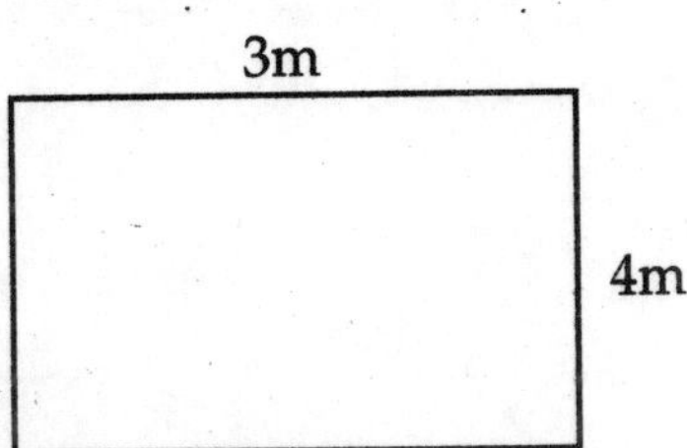

Area of Rectangle = length × breadth
= 3m × 4m
= $12m^2$

$12m^2$ is better read as 12 square metres rather than 12 metres squared.

A square metre is a particular unit of area, which is equivalent to the area of the square that has a side length of 1 metre.

On the other hand, "Metre squared" is the same thing but is somewhat more general. You can specify area in any unit you want so long as you have length multipled by breadth.

❑

OTHER FIELDS

Q. 1 : What is the oldest mathematical puzzle?

Ans : The oldest mathematical puzzle is found in the oldest mathematical book *Ahmes Papyrus.*

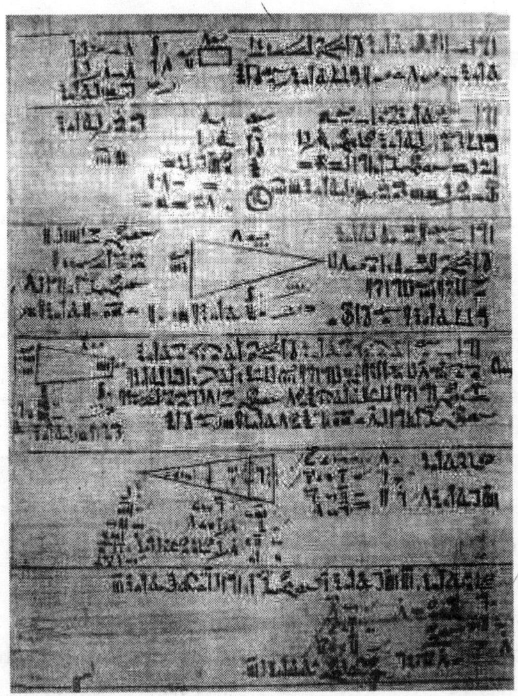

The Puzzle is—

"A man was going to St. Ives with his seven wives. Every wife had seven sacks and every sack had seven cats. Every cat had seven kittens. Kittens, Cats, Sacks and Wives, how many were going to St. Ives."

The answer to this puzzle comes out to 2801.

Man = 1
Wives = 7
Sacks = $7 \times 7 = 49$
Cats = $49 \times 7 = 343$
Kittens = $343 \times 7 = 2401$

Total = 2801

Here, 1, 7, 49, 343 and 2401 form GP.

Q. 2 : How can I tell the day of the year?

Ans : There is a formula that will help you to find the day of the year.

$$D = \left[\frac{23}{9}m + d + 4 + y + \frac{97}{100}z - 2\,(\text{if } m \geq 3)\right] \div 7$$

Here d = Date, m = Month, Y = Year and D = Day

RULE

(i) If $m < 3$, then take $z = y - 1$, otherwise $z = y$

(ii) if $m \geq 3$, subtract 2, otherwise not

(iii) Take only the integral part of division.

REMAINDER TABLE

Sun	Mon	The	Wed	Thu	Fri	Sat
0	1	2	3	4	5	6

Example 1 : On what day does 30th June 1974 fall?

Ans : Here m = 6, d = 30 and y = 1974

Since m 6 > 3, So z = y = 1974

Moreover, we have to subtract 2 at the end (Rule – 2)

$$D = \left[\frac{138}{9} + 30 + 4 + 1974 + \frac{191478}{400} - 2\right] \div 7$$

$= [15 + 30 + 4 + 1978 + 478 - 2] \div 7$

$= 357$

Since Remainder = 0

So 30th June 1974 falls on Sunday {See remainder Table]

Example 2 : On what day does 13th February 2006 fall?

Ans : $m = 2, \quad d = 13, \quad Y = 2006$

Since $m = 2 < 3$

So, $Z = y-1 = 2006 - 1 = 2005$

$\therefore D = [33 + 13 + 4 + 2006 + 486] \div 7$

$= 7 \times 36 + 1$

Since remainder = 1

Hence, 13th Feb 2006 falls on Monday.

Q. 3 : What is the highest prize in the field of mathematics?

Ans : Field Medal is certainly the highest prize in the field of mathematics. It is given to the mathematician who is below 40 years of age. It is considered equivalent to the Nobel Prize in the field of mathematics. John Charles Fields (1863–1962), a Canadian mathematician who endowed all his funds for an award given to the mathematician below 40 years of age for the excellent work in the field of mathematics.

This medal bears the image of Archimedes on one side of it. It was first given in 1936 in Oslo at the International Congress of mathematics.

a. Field Medal back image

b. Field Medal front image

Q. 4 : Why there is no Nobel prize in Mathematics?

Ans : There is no proper and authentic reason found so far about why there is no Nobel Prize in Mathematics.

The reason behind being no Nobel prize in Maths has some mythical reason, but there is no historical evidence to support it.

1. As per the story, G.Mittag-Leffler, a Swedish Mathematician had an affair with Sonya Kovalevskyaya, whom Alfred Nobel loved. Alfred Nobel found himself being cheated by the girl whom he loved most, decided not to include mathematics in the list of Nobel cateogry. Though unclaimed sources revealed that Nobel had planned to institute a prize in mathematics but had refrained because of his antipathy to Mittag–Leffler.

2. Another version of the story says that Nobel did not care much for mathematics, and that it was not considered a practical science from which humanity could benefit, and that was the reason that Nobel did not constitute a separate prize for mathematics.

Q. 5 : Are there any mathematicians who have been awarded the Nobel prize in other fields?

Ans : Yes, there are many mathematicians who have been recognised for their contribution in other fields by the Nobel Foundation. Here is the list of a few.

Name of Mathematicians	Year	Field
Lorentz	1902	Physics
Planck	1918	Physics
Einstein	1921	Physics
Bertrand Russell	1950	Isterature
Max Born/ Walther Bothe	1954	Physics
Tinbergen	1969	Economics
Kenneth Arrow	1972	Economics
Leonid Kantorovich	1975	Economics
John F. Nash	1994	Economics
Clive W.J. Granger	2003	Economics
Robert J. A Aumann	2005	Economics
Roger Myerson/Eric Maskin	2007	Economics

The above list is not full and final. There are many other mathematicians who have been awarded Nobel Prize in other fields. But to name them all is not possible.

Q. 6 : What does Trigonometry mean?

Ans : The word Trigonometry is derived from the Greek words Trigonon and Metron.

The word Trigonon means a triangle and the word metron means to measure. Hence Trigonometry means the science of measuring triangles. In broader sense, it is that branch of mathematics which deals with the measurement of the sides and angles of a triangle and the problems allied with angles.

Q. 7 : If B and Q are the acute angles such that Sin B = Sin Q, then why B = Q is written ?

Ans :

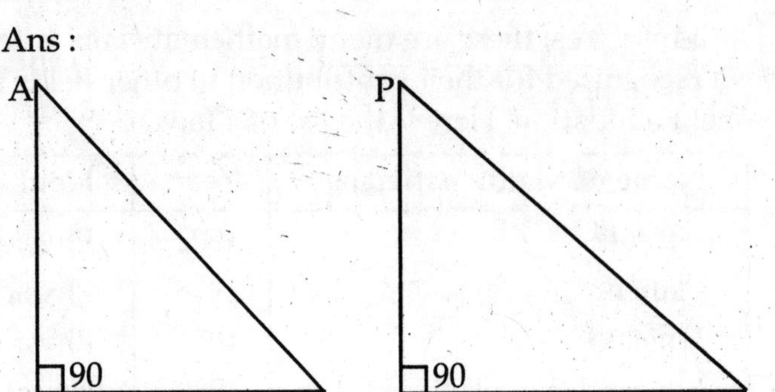

Let ABC and PQR be two right triangles with $\angle C$ and $\angle R$ be right angle.

$$\text{Sin}B = \frac{AC}{AB} \text{ and } \text{Sin}Q = \frac{PR}{PQ}$$

For SinB = SinQ

$$\frac{AC}{AB} = \frac{PR}{PQ} = K \text{ (say)—(1)}$$

$$\Rightarrow AC = KAB \text{ and } PR = KPQ\text{—(2)}$$

$$AB^2 = AC^2 + BC^2 \Rightarrow BC^2 = AB^2 - AC^2$$

$$\Rightarrow BC = \sqrt{AB^2 - K^2AB^2}$$

$$\Rightarrow BC = \sqrt{AB^2(1-K^2)}$$

Again, in ΔPQR

$$RQ = \sqrt{PQ^2 - PR^2}$$

$$= \sqrt{PQ^2 - K^2PQ^2}$$

$$= \sqrt{PQ^2(1-K^2)}$$

$$\frac{BC}{QR} = \frac{AB\sqrt{1-K^2}}{PQ\sqrt{1-K^2}} = \frac{AB}{PQ} \text{---(3)}$$

$$(1) \Rightarrow \frac{AB}{PQ} = \frac{AC}{PR} \text{---(4)}$$

From (3) and (4) we have,

$$\frac{AB}{PQ} = \frac{AC}{PR} = \frac{BC}{QR}$$

$$\Rightarrow \Delta ABC \sim \Delta PQR$$

$$\Rightarrow \angle B = \angle Q$$

Q. 8 : Prove the following result :

(a) $\text{Sin}^2\theta + \text{Cos}^2\theta = 1$

(b) $\text{Sec}^2\theta - \tan^2\theta = 1$

(c) $\text{Cosec}^2\theta - \cot^2\theta = 1$

Ans :

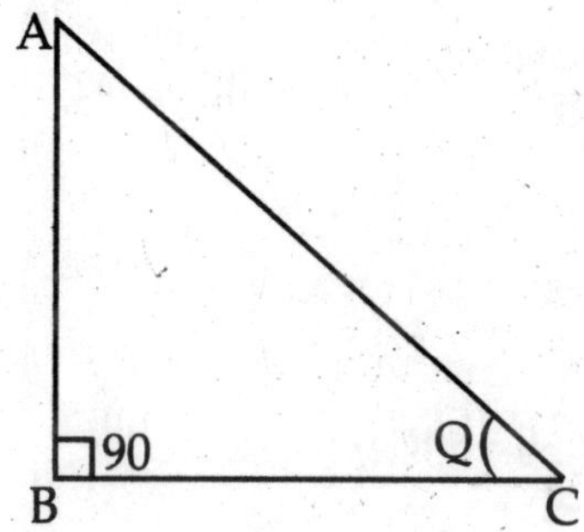

In $\Delta ABC, \angle B = 90^\circ$ and $\angle ACB = \theta$

$$\text{Sin}\theta = \frac{AB}{AC}, \ \text{Cos}\theta = \frac{BC}{AC}, \ \tan\theta = \frac{AB}{BC}$$

$$\text{Cosec}\,\theta = \frac{AC}{AB},\ \text{Sec}\theta = \frac{AC}{BC},\ \text{Cot}\theta = \frac{BC}{AB}$$

$\Rightarrow$ 1. $\text{Sin}^2\theta + \text{Cos}^2\theta$

$$= \frac{AB^2}{AC^2} + \frac{BC^2}{AC^2}$$

$$= \frac{AB^2 + BC^2}{AC^2}$$

$$= \frac{AC^2}{AC^2}$$ [$AB^2 + BC^2 = AC^2$; Pythagoras Theorem]

$= 1$

2. $\text{Sec}^2\theta - \tan^2\theta$

$$= \frac{AC^2}{BC^2} - \frac{AB^2}{BC^2}$$

$$= \frac{AC^2 - AB^2}{BC^2}$$ [$\because AB^2 + BC^2 = AC^2$]

$$= \frac{BC^2}{BC^2} = 1$$

3. $\text{Cosec}^2\theta - \cot^2\theta$

$$= \frac{AC^2}{AB^2} - \frac{BC^2}{AB^2}$$

$$= \frac{AC^2 - BC^2}{AB^2}$$ [$AB^2 + BC^2 = AC^2$]

$$= \frac{AB^2}{AB^2}$$

$$= 1$$

Q. 9 : Is it possible to find the trigonometric ratios of $0°, 30°, 45°, 60°, 90°$ with the help of geometry?

Ans : Yes, the trigonometric table can be constructed easily by using some elementary knowledge of Geometry.

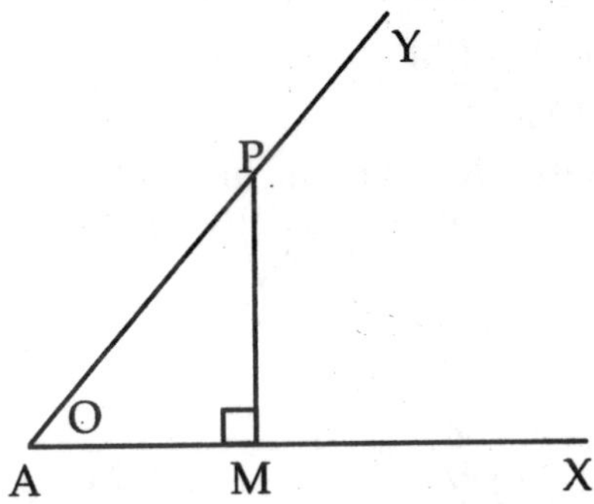

Let $\angle XAY = \theta$ be an acute angle and let P be a point on its terminal side AY. Draw $PM \perp AX$

In ΔPAM

$$\text{Sin}\theta = \frac{PM}{AP} \quad \text{Cos}\theta = \frac{AM}{AP} \text{ and } \tan\theta = \frac{PM}{AM}$$

The angle $\angle A = \theta$ becomes smaller and smaller, when the line segment PM also becomes smaller and smaller and when $\theta = 0$, PM coincides with M. For $PM = 0 \Rightarrow AP = AM$

$$\text{Sin}0° = \frac{PM}{AP} = \frac{0}{AP} = 0$$

$$\text{Cos}0° = \frac{AM}{AP} = \frac{AP}{AB} = 1$$

$$\tan 0° = \frac{PM}{AP} = \frac{0}{AP} = 0$$

Similarly, with the increase in θ the line segment AM becomes smaller and smaller and when $\theta = 90$ the point M will coincide with A.

AM = 0 and AP = PM

$$\text{Sin}90^\circ = \frac{PM}{AP} = \frac{PM}{PM} = 1$$

$$\text{Cos}90^\circ = \frac{AM}{AP} = \frac{0}{AP} = 0$$

$$\tan 90^\circ = \frac{PM}{AM} = \frac{PM}{0} = \infty$$

Trigonometric Ratio of 30° and 60°

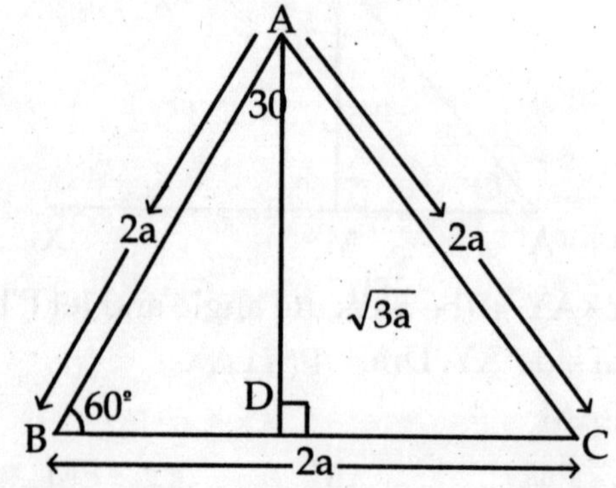

Let ABC be an equilateral triangle with each side equal to 2a

AB = BC = AC= 2a

$\angle A = \angle B = \angle C = 60^\circ$

Drop $AD \perp BC$

$\Rightarrow BD = CD = a$

In ΔABD,

$AD^2 = AB^2 - BD^2$

$= (2a)^2 - (a)^2$

$= 4a^2 - a^2 = 3a^2$

$AD = \sqrt{3a^2} = \sqrt{3}a$

Now,

$$\text{Sin}60^\circ = \frac{AD}{AB} = \frac{a\sqrt{3}}{2a} = \frac{\sqrt{3}}{2}$$

$$\text{Cos}60^\circ = \frac{BD}{AB} = \frac{a}{2a} = \frac{1}{2}$$

$$\tan 60^\circ = \frac{AD}{BD} = \frac{\sqrt{3a}}{a} = \sqrt{3}$$

Similarly, $\text{Sin}30^\circ = \frac{BD}{AB} = \frac{a}{2a} = \frac{1}{2}$

$$\text{Cos}30^\circ = \frac{AD}{AB} = \frac{\sqrt{3a}}{2a} = \frac{\sqrt{3}}{2}$$

$$\tan 30^\circ = \frac{BD}{AD} = \frac{a}{\sqrt{3a}} = \frac{1}{\sqrt{3}}$$

Trigonometric Ratio for 45°

Let ABC be an isosceles right triangle with AB = BC and $\angle C = 90^\circ$

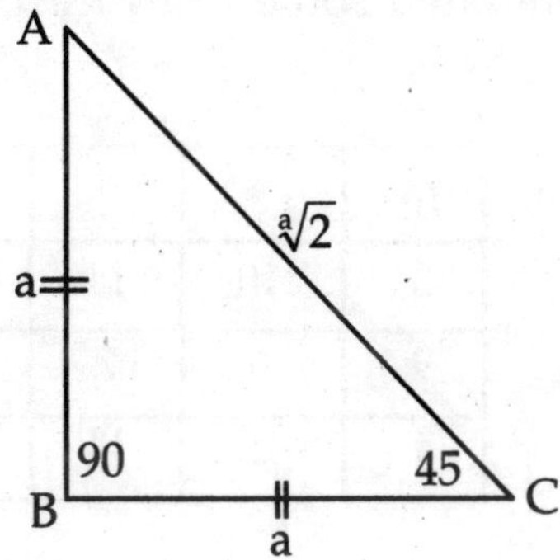

Let BC = AB = a

$$AC^2 = \sqrt{a^2 + a^2} = a\sqrt{2}$$

$$\text{Sin}45^\circ = \frac{AB}{AC} = \frac{a}{a\sqrt{2}} = \frac{1}{\sqrt{2}}$$

$$\text{Cos}45^\circ = \frac{BC}{AC} = \frac{a}{a\sqrt{2}} = \frac{1}{\sqrt{2}}$$

$$\tan 45^\circ = \frac{AB}{BC} = \frac{a}{a} = 1$$

Q. 10 : What is a magic square?

Ans : A square shaped mystical figure with some number associated with it in such a way that the sum of the numbers in each row, in each column, and in each major diagonal is the same.

It was discovered during 2000 BC by **Yu**, a Chinese Emperor. During the reign of Yu the great, he encountered two animals that were said to have magical power, a tortoise and a dragon horse. On the back of the tortoise was a pattern or symbol now known as the *loṣu* which represented a square array of numbers. Those numbers were first depicted by knots tied in strings, with white knots for odd numbers and black knots for even. During the 13th century, a mathematician Yang Hui, actually began to study magic squares referred to as vertical and horizontal diagrams. Yang Hui also generated some rules for constructing magic squares.

16	3	2	13
5	10	11	8
9	6	7	12
4	15	14	1

Here $16 + 3 + 2 + 13 = 34$
$5 + 10 + 11 + 8 = 34$
$9 + 6 + 7 + 12 = 34$
$4 + 15 + 14 + 1 = 34$
] Horizontal Sum

$$\left.\begin{array}{l}16 + 5 + 9 + 4 = 34\\ 3 + 10 + 6 + 15 = 34\\ 2 + 11 + 7 + 14 = 34\\ 13 + 8 + 12 + 1 = 34\end{array}\right]\text{Vertical Sum}$$

$$\left.\begin{array}{l}16 + 10 + 7 + 1 = 34\\ 4 + 6 + 11 + 13 = 34\end{array}\right]\text{Diagonal Sum}$$

Q. 11 : How can I prove 1 = 2 ?

Ans : We have

$$\frac{-1}{1} = \frac{1}{-1}$$

$$\Rightarrow \sqrt{\frac{-1}{1}} = \sqrt{\frac{1}{-1}}$$

$$\Rightarrow \sqrt{\frac{i^2}{1}} = \sqrt{\frac{1}{i^2}}$$

$$\Rightarrow \frac{i}{1} = \frac{1}{i}$$

$$\Rightarrow \frac{i}{2} = \frac{1}{2i} \text{(Dividing by 2)}$$

$$\Rightarrow \frac{i}{2} + \frac{3}{2i} = \frac{1}{2i} + \frac{3}{2i} \left[\text{Adding } \frac{3}{2i} \text{ both sides}\right]$$

$$\Rightarrow \frac{i^2}{2} + \frac{3}{2} = \frac{1}{2} + \frac{3}{2} \text{ [Multiplying both sides by i]}$$

$$\Rightarrow \frac{-1}{2} + \frac{3}{2} = \frac{1}{2} + \frac{3}{2}$$

$$\Rightarrow \frac{2}{2} = \frac{4}{2}$$

$$\Rightarrow 1 = 2$$

This impossible work can be made possible by one more method. Let us learn the method, Later we shall discuss the fallacy behind this proof.

Suppose $a = b$

$\Rightarrow a \times a = a \times b$ [Multiplying both sides by a]

$\Rightarrow a^2 + a^2 = a^2 + ab$ [Add a^2 both sides]

$\Rightarrow 2a^2 - 2ab = a^2 + ab - 2ab$ [Subtract 2ab from both sides]

$\Rightarrow 2a^2 - 2ab = a^2 - ab$

$\Rightarrow 2\ (a^2 - ab) = 1\ (a^2 - ab)$

$\Rightarrow 2 = 1$

Now the question is—**where is the mistake?** We all know that "any number when divided by number itself gives the quotient 1, except in the case $0 \div 0$".

In the beginning $a = b$ has been supposed.

Now come to the stage where we have cancelled $a^2 - ab$ by $a^2 – ab$. Since $a^2 - ab$ ($= a^2 - a.a = a^2 - a^2 = 0$) is divided by $a^2 - ab$ ($= 0$) which is against the hypothesis.

Q. 12 : Find the mistake in the given proof.

Re 1 = 100 P

and 1 Paise = $\dfrac{\text{Rs } 1}{100}$

Now; 10 Paise × 10 Paise = 100 Paise

$$\Rightarrow \text{Rs}\frac{1}{10} \times \text{Rs}\frac{1}{10} = \text{Rs } 1$$

$$\Rightarrow \text{Rs}\frac{1}{100} = \text{Rs } 1$$

$\Rightarrow$ 1 Paise = Rs 1

Ans : **Mistake :** 10 Paise × 10 Paise = 100 is wrong. It should have been 10 paise × 10 = 100 paise. This simple difference in writing brings the mathematical fallacy.

Q. 13 : Find the mistake :

We know $\sqrt{a} \times \sqrt{b} = \sqrt{ab}$

$\Rightarrow \sqrt{9} \times \sqrt{16} = \sqrt{144}$

$\Rightarrow 3 \times 4 = 12$ is true

Now take the case of negative numbers

$\sqrt{-9} \times \sqrt{-9} = \sqrt{-9 \times -9}$

$\Rightarrow 3i \times 3i = 9$

$\Rightarrow 9i^2 = 9$

$\Rightarrow i^2 = 1$

$\Rightarrow -1 = 1 \quad [\because i^2 = -1]$

Ans : **Fallacy :** $\sqrt{a} \times \sqrt{b} = \sqrt{ab}$ is true only if a and b are positive integers. In case of any number taken to be negative, the above relation stands invalid.

Q. 14 : Identify the mistake :

We know $\frac{1}{4} > \frac{1}{8}$

$\Rightarrow \left(\frac{1}{2}\right)^2 > \left(\frac{1}{2}\right)^3$

$\Rightarrow \log\left(\frac{1}{2}\right)^2 > \log\left(\frac{1}{2}\right)^3$ [Taking log on both sides]

$\Rightarrow 2\log\frac{1}{2} > 3\log\frac{1}{2} \, [\log a^{m^n} = n \log a^m]$

$\Rightarrow 2 > 3$

Ans : Remember, logarithm of any number is taken only when two values are equal and one of them is unknown. Taking log in inequalities problem is not valid.

Q. 15 : Find the fallacy :

We know, $16 - 36 = 25 - 45$

Add $\frac{81}{4}$ both sides

$16 - 36 + \frac{81}{4} = 25 - 45 + \frac{81}{4}$

$$\Rightarrow (4)^2 - \left(2\times 4\times \frac{9}{2}\right) + \left(\frac{9}{2}\right)^2 = (5)^2 - 2\times 5\times \frac{9}{2} + \left(\frac{9}{2}\right)^2$$

$$\Rightarrow \left(4-\frac{9}{2}\right)^2 = \left(5-\frac{9}{2}\right)^2$$

$[a^2 - 2ab + b^2 = (a - b)^2]$

$$\Rightarrow 4-\frac{9}{2} = 5-\frac{9}{2}$$

$$\Rightarrow 4 = 5$$

Ans : **Mistake :** if $a^2 = b^2$

$$\Rightarrow a = \pm b$$

$$\text{or } a^2 - b^2 = 0$$

$$\Rightarrow (a+b)(a-b) = 0$$

$$\Rightarrow a = -b \text{ or } a = b$$

$$\text{Here } \left(4-\frac{9}{2}\right)^2 = \left(5-\frac{9}{2}\right)^2$$

$$\Rightarrow 4-\frac{9}{2} \neq 5-\frac{9}{2} \text{ instead } \frac{1}{4} = \frac{1}{4}$$

brings the fallacy proving impossible into possible.

Q. 16 : Prove 0 = 1 and find out the mistake which helps in proving this result.

Ans : Step 1 : $(n + 1)^2 = n^2 + 2n + 1$

Step 2 : $(n + 1)^2 - (2n + 1) = n^2$

Step 3 : $(n + 1)^2 - (2n + 1) - n(2n + 1) = n^2 - n(2n + 1)$

Step 4 : $(n + 1)^2 - (2n + 1)(1 + n) = n^2 - n(2n + 1)$

$$\text{Step 5 : } (n+1)^2 - (2n+1)(n+1) + \frac{(2n+1)^2}{4}$$

$$= (n)^2 - n(2n+1) + \left(\frac{2n+1}{4}\right)^2$$

Adding $\left(\frac{2n+1}{4}\right)^2$ both sides

Step 6 : $\Rightarrow \left[(n+1)-\left(\frac{2n+1}{2}\right)\right]^2 = \left[n-\left(\frac{2n+1}{2}\right)\right]^2$

Step 7 : $\Rightarrow n+1-\left(\frac{2n+1}{2}\right) = n-\frac{2n+1}{2}$

Step 8 : $\Rightarrow n+1=n$

Step 9 : $\Rightarrow n-n=1$

Step 10 : $\Rightarrow 0=1$

Ans : **Mistake :** It occurs in step 7, if $x^2 = y^2 \Rightarrow x = y$ is the wrong step, because for $x^2 = y^2 \Rightarrow x = \pm y$

❑

BIBLIOGRAPHY

1. Fascinating Fibonacci : Trudi Hammel Garland
2. Mathematical Mystery Tour : Mark Wahl
3. Dictionary of Mathematics : James and James
4. History of Mathematics : D.E. Smith (Vol. 1 and 2)
5. Mac Tutor Archive (www.history.mcs.st-andrews.ac.uk)
6. www.members.aol.com/Jeff570
7. Prentice Hall Encyclopedia of Mathematics.
8. History of Mathematics—F. Cajori
9. Mathematics—David Bergamini
10. Maths Traveller—Clawson
11. Encyclopedia of Mathematics—Griesbach/Taylor
12. Mathematical Mysteries—Clawson
13. Everyday Mathematics
14. A new look at Numbers—JN Sharma
15. Out line of the History of Mathematics—R.C. Archibald.
16. Higher Algebra—Halls and Knight
17. A school Geometry—Halls and Stevens
18. Mathematical Magic—RK Thakur
19. High School Mathematics—MIR Publications
20. गणित का इतिहास—डा. ब्रज मोहन

❑❑❑